Gemstone Carving

Gemstone Carving

MARTIN WALTER

CHILTON BOOK COMPANY · Radnor, Pennsylvania

Library of Congress Cataloging in Publication Data

Walter, Martin.
　　Gemstone carving.

　　(Chilton's creative crafts series)
　　1.　Gem carving.　　I.　Title.
NK5525.W34　1977　　　736'.2　　　76-27650
ISBN 0-8019-6192-0
ISBN 0-8019-6193-9 pbk.

1 2 3 4 5 6 7 8 9 0　　6 5 4 3 2 1 0 9 8 7

To Marga, Michael and Robert

Preface

When I started to carve there was no single source of information I could find to set me on my way or to tell me what equipment to acquire. As a result, I did a lot of fumbling and stumbling and also wasted a lot of money unnecessarily. To spare my fellow enthusiasts some of these tribulations is one of the main aims of this book. I do realize that relatively few of my readers will execute all the tasks enumerated here. For this reason I have treated each chapter so that it can stand by itself as an independent unit. I highly recommend, however, that projects be undertaken in the order in which they appear as they follow each other logically, and tools and skills acquired in earlier undertakings will be needed in later enterprises. It is my secret hope that readers of this book will do better work than any which has been done before. While this may only be a chimerical dream, I wish sincerely that everyone who is going to read this book will get as much enjoyment from his or her endeavours as I had putting this book together.

Acknowledgments

Much friendly assistance was given to me during the preparation of the manuscript for this book. My wife contributed many helpful suggestions and did much of the typing. She also put up with me patiently while I struggled for nearly a year to complete all the various projects. My friend, Joe Rothstein, posed for some of the pictures and took some of the others. Mrs. Vivian Finger also contributed a number of photos, both in black and white and in color. Mrs. Ruth Saul corrected the manuscript and offered much useful advice. To all these kind helpers I should like to express my sincere gratitude.

Contents

List of Illustrations

Gemstone Carving

Introduction

It is natural for a lapidary who has mastered the fundamentals of his craft to look for new worlds to conquer. Are there such new worlds? The simplest way to answer this question is to look back on the history of lapidary work. We will be surprised to find that a graph depicting it is not a smoothly ascending curve, but a jagged line, the highest peaks of which are in the past—some in the very distant past. We will, to our astonishment, find also that more important work was done long ago than is being produced now. Everyone is aware, of course, that working with stone goes back a long way, but how long will be another surprise.

Findings in Olduvai Gorge and on the Serengeti Plains of Africa prove that man worked with stone at least 500,000 years ago. Also, excavators have produced proof that as far back as the Aurignacian period of stone age culture, which lasted from 40,000 to 15,000 B.C., man did creditable carvings in stone. This statement is verified by the fact that statuettes of fertility goddesses dating from the Aurignacian period have been discovered. The most famous of these, found at Willendorf in Austria and, therefore, named the "Venus of Willendorf," was executed in hard limestone. Another nearly as well known and similar figure, done in soapstone (steatite), turned up in a cave near Mentone, Italy.

In spite of the fact that these figurines may be anywhere from 42,000 to 17,000 years old, they show that their creators weren't novices. They display considerable technical skill and artistic know-how. From the fact that similar objects from this period have been found, and are still turning up in quite a few places, often at great distances from each other, we may assume that a fairly sophisticated lapidary technique was already widely disseminated at this early period.

Even so, the first peak of lapidary achievement of which we have definite knowledge comes somewhat as a surprise, like a wall of water resulting from the floodgate of a dam being unexpectedly opened. It occurred in Mesopotamia in the valleys of the Euphrates and the Tigris, where Sumerian and Hittite carvers, starting about 3,000 B.C., did work of such phenomenal skill that it probably has never been excelled. Their main products

1

were incised seals—mostly cylinder seals. These gemstone cylinders, made from soapstone, carnelian, lapis lazuli, and aventurine, to name but a few of the most popular materials, are from 1¼″ to 1½″ (31.75mm to 38.10mm) high, from ½″ to 1″ (12.70mm to 25.40mm) in diameter, pierced along the long axis, and carved with most intricate designs, including cuneiform writings. There are probably only a handful of people working today who, with electric motors, arbors of the most exacting construction, diamond points and magnifying lenses at their command, can equal this work. Whether these same people have the artistry and sense of design which seem innate in the carvers of ancient times is another question.

Thousands of these seals have been found, and probably any man of some standing owned at least one. This gives us an idea of the magnitude and importance of the lapidary accomplishment of that period. Further testimony to this has been found in the form of carvings in the round—beads, gem inlays, and other decorative objects of gemstone. The best known of these, a bull's head decoration on a harp and a statue of a ram fastened to a stylized tree, were excavated at Ur by Sir Leonard Woolley. They were found among other treasures in the grave of Queen Shubad which dates from 2,300 B.C.

The cylinder seals and other remarkable works of lapidary art were produced all over Mesopotamia down to, at least, 400 B.C. They were exported as far East as the Indus Valley, and as far West as the Island of Crete.

Simultaneously, and probably influenced by the Mesopotamians, gem carving and cutting reached great heights in Egypt. There, the most common products were the scarabs—oval shaped cabochon-like carvings—which were connected with the cult of the dead. Their rounded backs showed a stylized beetle shape. On the flat side, they bore hieroglyphic inscriptions which varied from prayers for the dead to records of memorable events. Most of these scarabs are about ¾″ (19.05mm) in length, but there are 3″ (76.2mm) and 4″ (101.60mm) long examples extant. Other gemstone objects of great beauty, testifying to incredible skill, were created. Beads by the thousands were produced in all sizes and shapes, very regular and well polished. Cloisonné work of gemstones set into gold was apparently very popular. It was the scarab though which, being easily portable, spread the influence of Egyptian lapidaries into Greece and Italy.

Greece, which since early antiquity had produced some notable gold work, had no lapidary industry to speak of until about the 6th century B.C. Homer, who wrote in the 8th century B.C., never once mentions gemstones. There were a few very fine carvings and seals found on Crete predating the cataclysm which destroyed the Mycenaean civilization about 1,400 B.C.; but then there is a hiatus in lapidary endeavor until the 6th century when an interest in the art reawakened.

At first, the gem carver's work was mostly in the form of stamp seals showing a strong influence of the Mesopotamian and Egyptian styles. By the 4th century B.C., the style, however, was all Greek, and the emphasis changed from intaglio to cameo work. Alexander the Great (356–323 B.C.), of whom quite a few cameo likenesses exist, according to Pliny, gave the gem carver Pyrgoteles a monopoly to execute his picture on gems "including emerald."

Cameo cutting, with a Greek accent, remigrated to Egypt. Alexandria was for a long time a center of this art. Among the most memorable creations of this period is the Farnese Cup, so called because later on it was owned by the Farnese family in Italy. It betrays its Egyptian origin by including among the figures depicted on it, a picture of the goddess Isis, and betrays its date by the profile of a woman who looks suspiciously like a well-known portrait of Cleopatra.

Cameo cutting thereafter was centered in Rome where it flourished during the first centuries before and after Christ. This was a period when gems, gem carvings, and vessels made of gemstone were used lavishly. Pliny the Elder (Gaius Plinius Secundus, 23–79 A.D.), who wrote an elaborately researched work on natural history, mentions practically all the gemstones we are working with today, including diamond and opal. While Pliny was very well informed and showed great insight in most matters concerning gemstones, he also committed a few colossal blunders, the most celebrated of which is his report about diamonds. He claimed that a diamond would not break if it was laid on an anvil and hit by a hammer. Subsequent naturalists copied this information which was not discredited until the 15th century, and may have resulted in the destruction of a great many diamonds.

The decline of the Roman Empire, which coincided with its division into two parts— the one in the west governed by Rome, the other governed by Byzantium—brought about a decided slowing down of lapidary endeavor in the western half, while the eastern area turned to Asian influences and sources for its gem work. Central and Southern Europe were in turmoil much of the time as Germanic tribes pushed south and westward. This was not the sort of atmosphere in which lapidary work would flourish. Gold and silversmith work was still in demand for adornment of the nobility and for ceremonial vessels and reliquaries for the church. But the gemstones we see in these sometimes very beautiful pieces show some very crudely worked pebbles, badly polished, or else reused gemstones pried out of their original settings. Among these are quite a few cameos of the Augustan period.

Even as the practice of the lapidary craft deteriorated in most of Europe, it saw a revival in Spain where the Arab conquerors, who held most of the peninsula for several hundred years, reintroduced it by bringing in craftsmen from the East. When the Moors were gradually expelled, from the 11th to the 13th century, the practitioners of the art also were driven out. They migrated to France and the Netherlands where they prospered.

This was due, in part, to the demand for a richer and more refined way of life which was growing in Europe. It had been ignited by views of the luxury the crusaders had seen in Asia Minor and the Holy Land, and fueled by the rapidly growing prosperity of the towns and cities. A guild of lapidaries was founded in Paris toward the end of the 13th century and another shortly thereafter in Nürnberg. One of the members of this body was Johann Gutenberg of Bible fame, who was a skilled gem and cameo cutter.

This was probably the time when gem cutting was established as a local industry in Idar-Oberstein and other places like Waldkirch near Freiburg in Germany, and Royat in France. We know that the large water-driven sandstone wheels, which were used in Idar-Oberstein until fairly recently, were developed during the 14th century. It was also during this period (late 14th and early 15th centuries) that diamonds became fashionable in Europe. Up to then, because diamonds were so difficult to work, lapidaries had contented themselves with polishing them more or less in the shape in which they were found. Now improved methods made it possible to apply a more refined technique. A man named Louis de Berquem is credited with inventing the fashion of cutting which, in a somewhat modified and improved form, is practiced to this day.

But since there was no knowledge of optics, many diamonds, even though they were cut in the new way, were not very attractive. Benvenuto Cellini reports in his memoirs that no one knew as well as he how to improve a diamond by backing it with colored metal foil. Cellini, who worked during the 16th century, was a witness to the highest peak the lapidary art achieved in Europe. The princes of the Italian city states vied with rulers all over Europe to commission the most splendid works for adornment of their persons and their banquet tables. The dignitaries of the church tried to outdo them by ordering reliquaries and other vessels to enhance their splendid churches. Many of these were carved from huge quartz crystals from the Swiss Alps, others were reworked vessels cut for use on Roman tables during the time of the Caesars, and still others were the results of importations of gemstones from the New World. A splendid example of the latter is the famous emerald unguent jar cut by Dionisio Miserone in the early 16th century for the Hapsburgs. It was at this time that the Wittelsbach dukes in Bavaria collected most of the splendid works which may be seen at the Schatzkammer in Munich.

By the end of the 16th century and the beginning of the 17th century, European cutters were further advanced than their colleagues in India (even though the Indian princes imported "ringers" from Europe) as far as diamond cutting was concerned. Witness to this is Jean Baptiste Tavernier (1605–1689), who made six extended trips to the Orient to buy gemstones, both rough and cut, and who tells about the splendor of the gem collections he saw in the palaces of the Moghul rulers of India. The lapidaries of their courts had a preference for very light colored or white jade, which they cut into paper-thin vessels of great beauty and encrusted with gold, rubies, and emeralds. Some of the best pieces created at the time are now a part of the Heber Bishop collection in the Metropolitan Museum of Art in New York. The Indian cutters who did this outstanding work may have come from China with the conquering Mongols, or have been descendants of a lapidary tradition based in Indonesia where G.H.R. von Koenigswald reports finding remnants of a rather advanced lapidary culture that existed during neolithic times.

China has an unbroken lapidary history for 4,000 years. It concentrates heavily on jade. The jade worked in China until about 200 years ago came from Turkestan in the form of nephrite. Only since that time was Burmese jadeite imported and worked. After the discovery of nephrite in Wyoming, much of it was exported to China and re-entered the United States as finished carvings.

While there may have been some contacts, tenuous though they may be among the lapidary cultures mentioned heretofore, a wholly independent branch of the lapidary art flourished in the Americas. Carvers working in Central and South America (Peru, British Honduras, Yucatán, and other parts of Mexico) created some wonderful projects. Again, the emphasis was on jade. Skillfully cut figurines, earplugs, plaques, masks, and other adornments have been found dated anywhere from 1,000 B.C. to the time of the Spanish Conquest. It is not definitely known where their jade came from. There are indications that as time went on it became scarcer. Later pieces were sometimes recut from older existing pieces, and the older (Olmec) works are generally larger than the objects of more recent times. Among the latter are some outstanding examples made of a mosaic of small pieces, apparently because there was no rough material in large enough sizes available.

Coming to more modern times—the 18th and 19th centuries—we find a decided decline in the work done in Europe. A lot of very showy and ambitious gemstone projects were still being created for the Indian princes, the Shahs of Iran, and the Sultans of Turkey. However, when looked at critically, this output is not as much of an achievement in the lapidary line as it appears to be at first glance. The pieces we see dazzle the eye because they are made by accomplished goldsmiths from wonderfully fine gem material, but the cutting of individual stones leaves much to be desired.

In Europe, the "last hurrah" was sounded at the court of the Russian Czars. They appreciated lapidary skill and were able to supply their cutters with fabulous rough materials from the Urals. The finest work these lapidaries did was the giant vases and huge columns surfaced with malachite, so precisely joined that the whole object looks as though cut from one piece of the gemstone. They also did some very fine smaller vases and other decorative objects, but toward the end of their output became too cute and overelaborate.

This brings us to today. Looking about us, we see a plethora of fine work being done. Cabochons and faceted stones, cut to very high standards, pour from the wheels of professionals all over the world. Elaborate carvings, made and sold by the gross, are available. Yet, there are very few stunning examples of the art which one would remember forever after having seen them once. There are no new departures. Why should this be so? The answer probably is that there is no incentive for professionals to go out of their way to experiment and waste untold hours on some lapidary task which may never return the investment of time and material lavished on it, when they have their hands full to satisfy an established market for well-made but nondescript goods. Thus, if there is going to be a new Golden Age of lapidary accomplishment, the work will have to come from amateurs.

Gem carving is a logical step forward for the experienced amateur lapidary, and in recent years more and more lapidaries have taken it up. It started small during the sixties, but has grown steadily as is evident by the ever-increasing number of articles, and offerings of new and improved tools in hobby magazines. The credit for this upsurge goes to a small band of pioneers, foremost among whom are Gordon S. Kennedy, Olive Colhour, and Ed and Leola Wertz. They have, of course, not invented gem carving or even rediscovered it, but they have opened the way to recognition of the fact that amateurs can do gem carving, and that it can be done with a relatively modest expenditure of money, by using ingenuity and limiting oneself to projects of reasonable scope. Dr. A. Worth Hobby, one of the very earliest pioneers whom few of us, however, can hope to emulate, has proven furthermore that given enough time, money, and talent, amateurs are able to rival the best work of the professionals.

It is hard to say what caused the popularity of carving among the amateurs. A good guess is that they are probably motivated by the same urge to create as that which made the Aurignacian mastodon hunter turn a hard limestone boulder into his version of female beauty, and by the somewhat more mundane, but no less admirable, desire to overcome difficulties just because they are there. From my own experience, I believe that there would be even more practitioners of the art if all the facts about it were more widely known. On seeing the elaborate Japanese and Chinese creations in rose quartz, jade, and carnelian with their many curlicues and dangling rings and chains, many people are apparently discouraged from even thinking about the possibility of entering the field. They would change their minds quickly if they knew that amateur and professional carving are two different ball games. An amateur cannot expect to possess the same facility as a professional carver for the simple reason that he does not have the time to go through years of apprenticeship repeating the same operations hundreds of times until they are second nature. Nor can he expend large amounts of money, as a rule, for outstanding material and large elaborate machinery like the professional, who has reasonable expectations to recover his outlays by selling the product.

The amateur, however, still has plenty of room in which to maneuver, and he, unlike his counterpart, can give his inventiveness and sense of beauty free rein to create whatever he likes within the limits of his ability and means. Thus, in the following instructions, no attempt is made to teach the best way of carving gemstones, but on how best to accomplish this within the limits imposed by circumstances on the average amateur.

As more and more people learn to cut and carve, an educated appreciative public will be established to encourage the creation of more outstanding work. As additional information and better tools become available to these new cutters, and as their numbers increase, there are bound to be among them people with the ambition, talent, and ability to do better work than has ever been done. To that happy prospect this book is dedicated.

1
Fundamentals of Carving

There are just a few preconditions which those who want to enter this rewarding avocation have to live up to. The first, and most important of these, is a good grounding in the basic techniques of gem cutting. This experience should cover, particularly, the handling of the more difficult materials such as jade and rhodonite, which are among the preferred gemstones for carving. A second requirement is ownership or ready access to standard lapidary machinery. A third is the availability, or possibility to acquire some additional cutting, sanding, and polishing tools for use in finer detail work. The fourth is the necessity to overcome the mental block which makes so many people believe that only the gifted with the ability to draw or paint can take up carving.

It has been my experience that the average man or woman who "cannot draw a straight line" does very well, even on his or her first attempt, at modeling three-dimensional objects. This opinion is unanimously shared by all the pioneers of amateur carving as can be readily ascertained from their writings. Another important fact is that anyone with experience in gem cutting seems to have little trouble recreating an existing three-dimensional model in suitable gemstone once he has been taught the principles. Anyone reading this can verify these statements by trial.

MATERIALS

There are a number of considerations to guide an amateur carver's choice of gem materials. Availability in chunks large enough to carve is one; ease of working is another; resistance to splintering, third; and price, fourth. There are others. For example, a man living where unakite is locally available will work with it by preference.

The only material about which there will not be an argument is nephrite. It is the carving medium par excellence, even though there may be wide variations in the qualities of nephrite from different localities. There may even be divergences in different areas of

6

the same boulder. It owes its popularity partly to the ease with which it abrades, and partly to its toughness which keeps it from splintering, permitting it to be worked to great thinness without danger of breaking. Another advantage is that it is available from many sources in sawed blocks.

Nephrite jade does have some drawbacks. It is one of the most inconsistent materials to polish. No one has yet come up with a "foolproof recipe" for getting a good finish on this material. There are certain universal facts, however, which apply to the handling of this finicky gem. Heat will help in the development of a good finish. This applies to sanding as well as to polishing. Often the finish obtained on a sanding cloth is so good that it cannot be improved. Hard leather, underlaid by a hard surface in conjunction with chromium oxide, or, in some cases, a mixture of chromium oxide and Linde A powder sometimes is the answer. Carbopol jelly (see section on clay models) mixed with 600 grit silicon carbide power applied to a wood lap, was used on some of the projects described in this book with satisfactory results. The mixture, which may be used dry for quite a while without being renewed, forms a glaze on the wood. Carbopol mixed with one micron (one thousandth of a millimeter) alumina also produces a good finish in some cases. When all else fails, diamond compounds (8000 and 14000 grit) usually can be relied on to come to the rescue.

Another disadvantage applies only to those who do not live in jade country. It is a fact of life that Eastern dealers, as a rule, do not carry jade in any variety or in the larger blocks, and particularly not in the lower price ranges, even though the situation seems to have improved a bit of late. Purchases by mail order from the West, on the other hand, are fraught with difficulties. There is an understandable reluctance of many dealers to enter into correspondence, answer questions, or send samples. Some, to be sure, are willing to ship on approval, but the postage both ways, in the case of returns, must be paid by the buyer. This runs into money since weights of several pounds are usually involved. This, on the other hand, offers the enticing angle that the need for purchasing jade is a persuasive argument for the necessity of taking that trip to the West which has been on your mind so long. As more and more people resort to carving, the nephrite supply in the East, no doubt, will improve in response to growing demand.

Difficulty in acquiring jade should not keep anyone from carving, since there are so many attractive materials other than jade available. On the assumption that anyone about to enter into carving should have been working at lapidary for some time, it may be assumed that he or she is in possession of a small hoard of cutting materials. Among these treasures there is bound to be more than one chunk suitable for carving. Often friends can be talked out of some of their rockpile. The following list enumerates gem materials in the order of my own personal preference. I would refuse to get into an argument with any carver establishing different priorities. Nor is the list anywhere near complete since, theoretically, any gem material is suitable for carving. It was mentioned earlier that even emerald has been used for the purpose of creating an ointment cup for a Hapsburg emperor during the sixteenth century. It is obviously not a suitable medium for an amateur. The items listed here have been chosen because they are commonly available in pieces large enough to carve, and at prices which are relatively reasonable.

Clay Models

I recommend that everyone who is interested in carving, particularly if there is no previous experience in creating three-dimensional objects, should start by executing small figures in clay as an encouraging introductory exercise. The clays used are the nonhardening varieties which go by such names as Plastelena, Plasticine and many others. They are obtainable in most stationery and variety stores and in practically all art supply houses. A

Gemstones

Material	Principal locations	Price range	Remarks
Nephrite	Wyoming, Alaska, British Columbia	reasonable to very expensive	
Rhodonite	U.S.A., Australia	reasonable	tends to undercut
Unakite	Virginia, New Jersey	inexpensive	technically a granite
Sodalite	Brazil, Canada	reasonable	hard to get in flawless chunks
Serpentine	worldwide	inexpensive to reasonable	comes in many colors
Tigereye	Africa	reasonable	
Malachite	Africa	expensive	grind and sand wet; dust dangerous
Obsidian	Western U.S.A., Mexico	inexpensive	very brittle—available in large chunks
Rose Quartz	Brazil	reasonable to expensive	fragile
Rutilated quartz	Brazil	reasonable to expensive	fragile
Agate Chalcedony Jasper	Brazil, Mexico, Western U.S.A.	inexpensive to reasonable	very tough—hard on tools

The following materials are so soft that they can be worked with steel tools. However, it is nearly impossible to preserve clean contoured lines when sanding and polishing because of this same lack of hardness.

Howlite	California	inexpensive	
Alabaster	Many states of U.S.A.	inexpensive	
Soapstone	worldwide	inexpensive	
Mexican Onyx	California, Mexico	inexpensive	a variety of calcium carbonate

good way to start is to use a small carving or a clay figurine as a pattern. Even from the very beginning there is the possibility that one of the figures may be good enough to be executed in gemstone. Therefore, it is recommended that the carver choose simple examples which are without deeply undercut recesses or thin protuberances. They should also be small enough so that the clay reproductions do not require internal stiffening. Later on, when we progress to more complicated forms, it may be necessary to mold the clay over armatures or skeletons of fairly thick, but flexible, aluminum wire. These are available in art and hobby shops.

In the beginning when the carver has little or no experience, it is advisable to start modeling shapes a little larger than the ones which will eventually be translated into gemstone. This is because the smaller the object being worked on, the greater the difference a little detail may make. Good measurements to start with are 2″ by 4″ by 6″ (50.80mm by 101.60mm by 152.40mm). There are small wooden modeling tools which can be bought in art stores which will help in the work. The modeling tools can, of course, be whittled at home, or a nail pushed into a piece of wood or a penknife will serve nearly as well.

When one of these larger figurines pleases its creator, it can then be reduced in size, possibly in more than one step, until a satisfactory model of suitable size for carving is achieved (see Fig. 1-1). At this stage of development, the newcomer shouldn't try to finish a shape in just one session. He will find, as I have discovered many times, that a figure which appeared "just beautiful" during the throes of first creation appears much

Fig. 1-1 Clockwise from center top: a large clay model of squirrel; a smaller clay version; the finished jade image.

less perfect in the sober light of the next morning. It is good to mull over the initial efforts for several days. After some experience has been gained in recreating three-dimensional figures, attempts should be made to work from pictures such as illustrations in magazines, books, and on postcards.

Sooner or later, most likely sooner, one of the models will look good enough to be carved in gemstone. This model should be of the exact size of the desired end-product. Next, the same figure should be recreated in the very same dimensions, but this time, instead of being built up or squeezed into shape, it is produced by starting with a block of clay and whittled away with a penknife to achieve the same final result. This will give valuable hints for using the saw for preforming. If the carver has a block of gem material which he intends to shape into a particular design, the clay block should first be molded into a likeness of the block of gem material, and then carved into the desired shape. If too much clay is carved away, occasionally in this operation it is alright to put it back as long as the carver is aware that when working in stone such correction is not possible.

The number of clay figurines required before one is suitable for carving depends on the individual. A minimum for the very talented is three: one larger figure, one in the dimensions to be carved, and one of the same size, whittled down. Folks without experience will probably want to do at least three or four of the larger figurines, and may need two or three repetitions of the same model in stepping down to carving size. The main thing is never to give up the ship. A consoling thought to sustain the beginner in the difficulties he is bound to encounter is that one can always assume the mantle of a modern sculptor and pretend that the misshapen results of one's efforts was intended to look that way. This will make the carver automatically a member of the avant-garde, with the resulting benefit of having to take fewer showers and getting higher prices should he or she decide to sell.

9

Carbopol Mixture

In the following text, there will be occasional references to Carbopol mixtures. Carbopol is a material manufactured by B.F. Goodrich for use in compounds such as face creams, shaving creams, etc. It will have to be purchased directly from B.F. Goodrich. A minimum purchase of five pounds of the powder is required by the manufacturer. Since the compound is inexpensive (about $3 per pound), it should not be difficult to get a few fellow lapidaries or gem club members to share the order. A pound will last the average cutter for the better part of a lifetime. We sent our request to B.F. Goodrich Chemical Co., 140 Sylvan Avenue, Englewood Cliffs, NJ 07632. The firm probably has offices in all large cities and it is advisable to call and find out whether it is possible to order the product locally.

Carbopol is a white powder which is dissolved in water (a heaping tablespoon to a quart of water). Then, a saturated solution of lye is made by stirring a teaspoon of the chemical into 4 oz. of water. The mixing is done in a glass or ceramic vessel using a glass or wooden instrument for stirring. Some of it will remain undissolved. Surplus may be dumped into a sink which is then flushed copiously with water. The lye solution is added to the Carbopol mixture and stirred thoroughly. This solution should be handled with great caution. The B.F. Goodrich people recommend use of a mixer similar to the ones which are employed for making cake doughs in home kitchens. However, a good stirring is all that is necessary. The mixture will contain a lot of air bubbles to start with. These will eventually rise to the surface and vanish, and then leave a clear jelly. A small amount of this jelly is mixed with either silicon carbide or any of the polishing powders. The jelly mixtures have the advantage of sticking much more tenaciously to the tools they are used on than water solutions of the same materials.

PROCEDURES

There are nine steps through which most carvings are taken. They usually follow each other in the order in which they are enumerated below.

Steps 1 and 2—Procuring Materials and Making a Clay Model

These first two steps are interchangeable. One may either make a model and then order material to fit it, or one may create the model to conform to material already on hand.

Step 3—Forming a Gemstone Blank

This step calls for the use of a slabbing saw if one is available or, in case of its absence, a trimsaw (see Chapter 2, Tools and Machinery). If a trimsaw is used, it should be at least 8″ (203.20mm) in diameter, preferably larger, and be equipped with a reliable vise. The saw is used to cut the blank. The sides of the blank should be at right angles and parallel to each other, and contain within their limits the dimensions required by the model.

Step 4—Sawing a Preform

The blank is then marked by superimposing on it the model or templates made from the model so that as much surplus material may be removed from it by sawing as can be managed. If the object is fairly large and sizable pieces have to be removed, a slabbing saw would be desirable for the first cuts.

Step 5—Initial Shaping

After sawing off as much material as possible, additional gemstone is ground away on the larger grindstones (8"—203.20mm—or over).

A limited amount of carving can be done by just the five steps mentioned so far. In this case, one would go directly from Step 5 to Steps 8 and 9 (sanding and polishing).

Step 6—Detail Carving

To create more elaborate carvings, the novice will need small tools and equipment to use for this purpose. Some of these, such as small grinding wheels, may be homemade; others, such as Mizzy wheels, will have to be bought.

Step 7—Drilling

While not used in every project, drilling is of utmost importance in others. Many of the tools and machines used for detail carvings are also employed in drilling.

Step 8—Sanding

Sanding for the first few projects can be accomplished on the regular equipment used for cabochon cutting. For more complicated carving, it will have to be done with small tools run on the flexible shaft, the point carver, the combination drill carver, or a regular carving setup. Some sanding may even be done by hand.

Step 9—Polishing

What has been said about sanding also applies to polishing. While sanding is necessary in all operations, polishing may be omitted occasionally; i.e., where a high gloss finish is not considered desirable.

SAFETY PRECAUTIONS

Working with stones can be a hazardous pastime in that certain rocks emit poisonous or otherwise harmful gases or dust. Since carvers must be familiar with these potential

Fig. 1-2 Safety goggles and respirator.

dangers from their previous lapidary experience, let me just say that the usual pitfalls facing a gem cutter are magnified by the fact that much larger masses are involved in the work. It is, therefore, recommended that participants should protect their lungs against inhaling flying dust and their eyes against the dangers of splinters. This is doubly important when dealing with the potentially poisonous copper materials such as malachite, which should always be worked as wet as possible. There are good dust masks and goggles available at most hardware stores, which give fair protection (see Fig. 1-2). It is preferable to be joshed for looking like an astronaut than to expose oneself to unnecessary risks. Working in well ventilated places is also helpful.

2
Tools and Machinery

GENERAL INSTRUCTIONS

Gem carving is different from the cutting of cabochons only by the fact that it creates more complicated shapes. Thus, it uses the same tools and methods for the most part, adding equipment only to work the smaller, less accessible, surfaces which are a result of the more involuted design. Methods, naturally, are also more or less the same. But there is a difference of opinion about whether it is better to use a flexible shaft or other movable point to do the carving on an object kept stationary, or whether it is preferable to carve with a stationary tool to which one brings the gem material. Good arguments may be offered for both sides. Obviously, if the block to be carved is too heavy to handle comfortably, the tools will have to be brought to it. This, though, is scarcely ever to be expected in amateur carving. On the other hand, there is the fact not to be neglected that the Oriental carvers have used stationary carving points for many centuries. So do the artists working at Corning Glass and other centers of highly skilled intaglio glass carving (see Glossary). This may just be due to tradition. It may be assumed that fine carving evolved from rough grinding by degrees. As the larger grinding devices were stationary, they evolved into smaller ones equally immovable.

Conservatism is naturally high in a craft which entails prolonged apprenticeship under masters who, in turn, were taught by men of long tradition. I myself prefer the stationary tool point for carving, but must concede that there are situations when the added flexibility of being able to move both the tool and the object may be a decided advantage. This applies particularly to sanding and even more so to polishing. These operations can often be performed best by holding the tool in a movable shaft in one hand and the object in the other, thus keeping the place being worked on visible at all times.

PURCHASING NEW MACHINERY

One of the great quandaries the beginning carver faces is what and how much new equipment to purchase. To help in this decision, I have devised a series of projects in ascending line of difficulty. In addition, they are arranged so that the first few undertakings require no new acquisitions; and the next few, only limited expenditures. The idea of this is to give beginning carvers a chance to find out how they like carving, and whether, and how deeply they want to commit themselves.

Even when the newcomer has decided "to stay with it," there is still a bewilderment of choices. A handy man, on the one hand, may content himself with converting a second-hand foot-powered sewing machine into a carver at a cost of $25 or less. While, on the other hand, a lucky plutocrat to whom money means little or nothing will have no trouble spending $1000 or more by buying all the gadgets in sight.

If either a flexible shaft tool or a point carving tool is already available, it may be adapted for carving or drilling by purchasing one of the diverse stands, which are on the market, to render these appliances stationary (see Fig. 2-1 and Fig. 2-2). A pipe clamp held in a bench vise could be utilized for this purpose, but care should be taken in this case not to crush the handpiece. If the would-be-carver has a true-running drill press or lathe, it may be drafted for this work; but remember that coolants and abrasive grits are involved in carving and they might ruin machinery not built to stand up to them unless special precautions are taken.

An economic way of building a carving setup is to rig up an arbor (ball bearing if possible), with a triple pulley on one end and a Jacob's chuck on the other, attached to a good electric motor of one-third or one-half horsepower (.25kw or .37kw). An even better, but

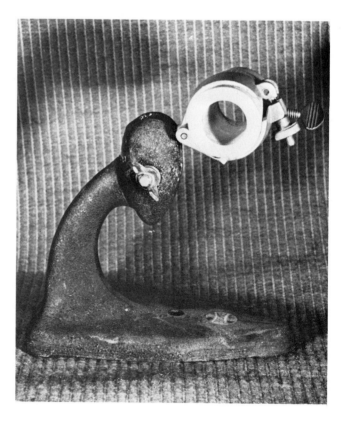

Fig. 2-1 A stand to hold the handpiece of a flexible shaft or point carver.

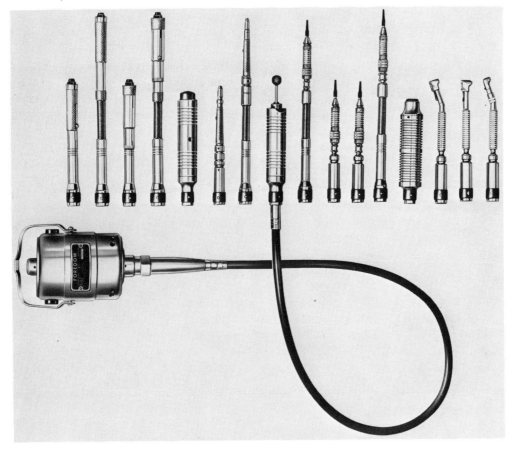

Fig. 2-2 A flexible shaft tool. (Courtesy Foredom Electric Co.)

more difficult to build, arrangement can be constructed by rigging two pillow block bearings with a suitable shaft. The triple pulley on this carver can be between the pillow blocks, leaving both ends available for tool holders.

The most economical carving machine of all is one based on a secondhand, foot-powered sewing machine, described in a short article by Charles Sims in the *Lapidary Journal*, October 1972. Forrest W. Pond has written a very fine little book, *How to Make and Use Gem Carving Tools*, in which he describes such constructions, including a multi-speed, multi-spindle arrangement which permits the operation of several carving shafts simultaneously, thus making it unnecessary to stop constantly to change carving points. The home-built setups, incidentally, are just the thing for mounting 6″ (152.40mm) silicon carbide wheels, small saws, and, as we shall see later, felt disks with the use of an adapter, so that they can be run vertically (see Fig. 2-3).

There are five firms making combination carvers and gem drills. They are Covington Engineering (see Fig. 2-4), P.D.Q. Manufacturing (see Fig. 2-5), Geode Industries (makers of the Viking Gem Drill—see Fig. 2-6), Frances Paul Crafts, Division of Crown Mfg. Co. (makers of the Pro-Carva Gem Drill—see Fig. 2-7), and Highland Park Mfg. Co. (see Fig. 2-8). These machines successfully perform many carving operations in addition to drilling, thus making it unnecessary to buy a separate drill. They are the ideal solution for anyone who is going to take his carving seriously and has only limited space.

Fig. 2-3 A homemade carving machine.

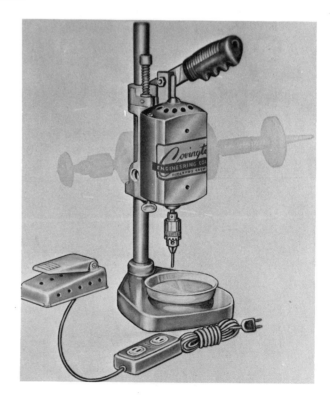

Fig. 2-4 Gem drill. (Courtesy
Covington Engineering)

Fig. 2-5 Gem drill. (Courtesy
P.D.Q. Lapidary Manufac-
turing)

Fig. 2-6 Viking gem drill.
(Courtesy Geode Industries)

A wide range of projects can be handled with the help of these combination machines. There may come a time, however, when one will want a separate carving setup and use the drill only for drilling. The answer to this would be the addition of one of the home-made carvers or a commercially built one (also by Crown Mfg. Co.), which has the advantage over the home product in that it can be tilted to any angle with a twist of a knob and has an electric speed control (see Fig. 2-9).

It should also be mentioned that there are compact, ultra-sonic drills on the market now which also do some carving. The least expensive of these are in the $800 to $900 range; a price which puts them out of the reach of most amateurs—Highland Park Mfg. Co., and Geode Industries carry them.

Here, as in all things, one gets what one pays for; and the better the equipment, the easier the work. Time spent in improvising equipment and tools could be used for actual carving. But, then, many people get as much fun out of employing their ingenuity to save their pocketbook as they do out of carving.

For the average novice who intends to take this thing seriously, an initial outlay of about $200 to $300 over the first couple of months is probably to be expected. This includes the purchase of a combination gem drill/carver. But practically any hobby requires the outlay of some money. One would expect to spend that much for a good set of golf clubs. There is one big difference in favor of the carving equipment though, for time spent with the golf clubs entails additional expenses and will at best result in some

Fig. 2-7 Pro-Carva gem drill.
(Courtesy Crown Mfg. Co.)

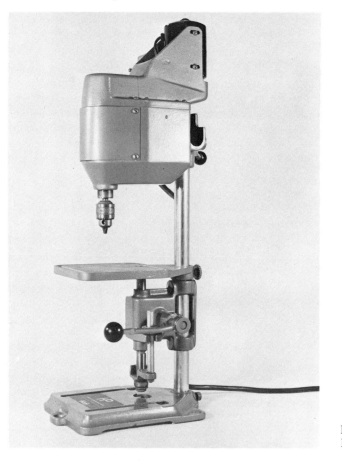

Fig. 2-8 Gem drill. (Courtesy
Highland Park Mfg. Co.)

Fig. 2-9 Rohlane Carver.
(Courtesy Crown Mfg. Co.)

pleasant memories. Time spent with carving equipment, on the other hand, will require very little additional outlay and create intrinsic values, not to speak of the enjoyment the carver experiences in creating.

USING CARVING MACHINERY

In the following it will be taken for granted that the operator is familiar with standard gem cutting procedure. Only new uses of standard machinery and the application of newly added equipment will be discussed.

Sawing

The lapidary appliance which takes on the greatest burden of new roles in carving is the saw. It is capable of removing fairly large amounts of gemstone in a much shorter time than it would take to abrade the same volume of material. Furthermore, some of the pieces thus cut off may be usable for cabochons, which is an advantage, particularly if beautiful and expensive stone is being carved.

As much of the sawing as possible should be done on an automatic slabbing saw (see Fig. 2-10). The use of the saw for this purpose is far from easy because there are no accu-

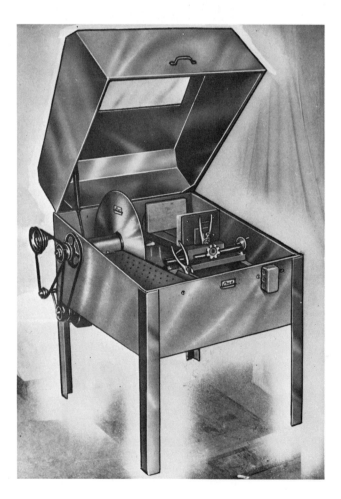

Fig. 2-10 A slabbing saw.
(Courtesy Covington Engineering)

Fig. 2-11 Lining up of saw cut with steel ruler.

rate sighting devices to assure the correct position of the block of material in relation to the saw blade. The adjustment must be done mostly by eye. However, a ruler held against the saw blade (parallel to the side opposite the vise) will indicate accurately the size of the slab about to be cut (see Fig. 2-11). Holding the ruler against the other side of the saw blade will indicate the line of cut for the remaining material. A carpenter's try square will also give some aid and comfort in lining up a block of gemstone at right angles to the saw blade, particularly if there is a previously sawn surface to refer to. The try square is most useful when sawing on a trimsaw, but it will be of assistance with a slabbing saw, also (see Fig. 2-12). With the latter, they are employed to line up the material in relation to the jaws of the vise holding it.

Mistakes can be held to a minimum by stopping the saw after it has been at work for a few seconds to check that the cut is on the right side of the mark, and as close to it as it should be. Another check after a short while is advisable to ascertain that all is well. In the beginning, it may be wise not to try and saw too closely, but rather to allow for some margin of safety. Remember this, too, when ordering your material.

It is extremely useful to know what distance the saw carriage of the slabbing saw travels on each turn of the crank. To find this out, one makes an initial cut, and then, for example, turns the crank six times. Another cut is taken and the width of the resulting slab is measured. This measure divided by six is the figure we want to find out. Knowing this will take the guesswork out of cutting identical blanks.

If a slabbing saw is not available, either a regular trimsaw or an overhead saw will have to be used. Of these, the regular trimsaw is preferable for cutting blanks and for trimming blanks into preforms. The saw used for this purpose should be at least 8″ (203.20mm) in diameter, but preferably larger. It should be equipped with a vise which holds the material securely and moves it forward in a straight line. Even so, it should not

Fig. 2-12 Lining up material at right angles to the saw blade.

be expected that a trimsaw will work as efficiently, nor be as trouble-free as a slabbing saw. Every effort should be made to find an owner of a slabbing saw who will for love or money custom-saw pieces where the resulting cut will be much more than 3″ (76.2mm) square.

For trimming blanks into preforms, the material very often has to be held by hand. When doing this, the thought that the saw is a delicate instrument should always be uppermost in the worker's mind. The saw will be ruined if its rim is twisted out of shape, and it will not be of much use anymore if its set (the increased thickness of the leading edge) is worn off.

There are certain rules to remember for hand-held sawing. The blank should have at least one level plane of sufficient size so that the sawer can hold it on the saw table without wobbling. The work should be fed slowly to the blade without forcing. The attention of the worker should be solely concentrated on what he is doing. If there are interruptions, or if he gets tired, sawing should be temporarily stopped. It is also important to remember when using the trimsaw in this manner, that a cut made with the material resting flat on the saw table will have a considerable slant. The cut will be much deeper at the table level than at the top of the gemstone. There are three methods to obtain a level kerf.

1. If the saw incision is exactly at right angles to the leading edge of the material, and if this leading edge is a straight line at table level, it may be evened out by tilting the block carefully.

2. If the top and bottom plane of the blank are parallel, a near level cut may be obtained by making an incision with one side of the material resting on the saw table. Then, when this bottom cut has reached the required depth, the material may be turned over

and the sawing continued in the same kerf until both incisions have reached the same depth. The center of the cut will be a little higher than either end.

3. The material may be rested on an angle iron or wedge of wood into which a slot has been sawed at 90 degrees to the longer edge, and wide enough to accommodate the saw blade (see Fig. 2-13). The sides of the wedge in Figure 2-14 are 2″ (50.80mm) and 3″ (76.20mm) long, but could be 2¹/₂″ (63.50mm) and 3³/₄″ (95.25mm), or 3″ (76.20mm) and 4¹/₂″ (114.30mm). They should form a right angle and the slot is in the center of the longer side. If an angle iron is not obtainable, a wooden wedge will serve. The material is aligned and firmly held on this wedge so that the line to be cut is exactly above the slot,

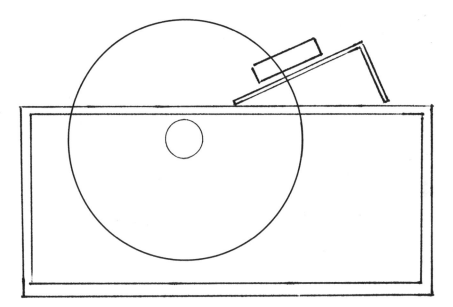

Fig. 2-13 Material being sawed on an angle iron.

Fig. 2-14 An angle iron with a slot for the saw blade.

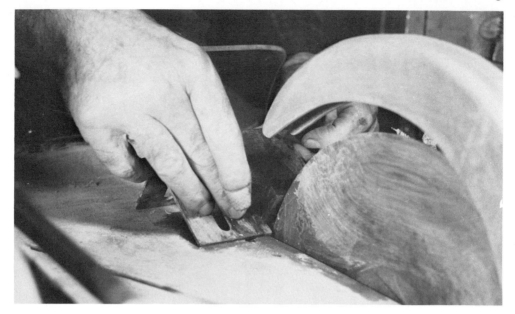

Fig. 2-15 Cutting jade resting on an angle iron.

which is then guided into the saw (see Fig. 2-15). If a rip fence (see Glossary) is available on the saw or if one can be rigged, it will make things easier.

The saw may, on occasion, be used to incise lines which form part of the design, or which will later be deepened by grinding. There are some small (1"—25.40mm—or less) diamond saw blades which come either on fixed mandrels (see Glossary), or may be mounted on changeable mandrels which are even better for this purpose (see Fig. 2-16).

Fig. 2-16 Small saw blades, factory and homemade.

Larger saws also may be used to do some abrading in places too narrow for the grind-stones. For this work the overhead saw is superior to the trimsaw because of the better visibility of the working area. If much grinding with the saw is to be done, several sawblades of exactly the same diameter and degree of wear can be bunched on the same shaft, thus improvising a thin diamond grindstone. The homemade carving machines about which we will hear later, can be rigged with this arrangement, but unless a good supply of water can be provided, it may do more harm than good.

Grinding

When all possibilities of using the saw to preform have been exhausted, the same wheels which customarily do the grinding of cabochons take over. The only difference be-tween cabochon procedure and carving is that the edges of the wheel are called into play. They are used as they are, or one of them is rounded off on purpose to facilitate the grind-ing of concave planes.

In this work, the outer edge of the wheel's periphery and the adjacent outer edge of the wheel's side are used, either singly or simultaneously. A great variety of curves can be cut by different slants of the rough in relation to the wheel. It may be necessary to "dress" (see Glossary) the grinding wheels frequently since we are working with relatively large masses. Some wear and tear on the grinding wheels may be avoided, however, by holding the material being worked on a tool rest for as much of the process as is tech-nically possible (see Fig. 2-17). This, in fact, may even dress the wheels to a certain ex-tent. The large wheels are naturally limited by their size from working out smaller details, and for this purpose, new tools have to be resorted to.

In shopping for these auxiliary appliances, it will be discovered that there are no lapidary wheels available between the smallest "large" wheel, which measures 6″

Fig. 2-17 Grinding gemstone held on a tool rest.

(152.40mm) in diameter and $1/2''$ (12.70mm) thick with a $1/2''$ (12.70mm) arbor hole, and the largest "small" wheel, which is $1''$ (25.40mm) in diameter, and from $1/16''$ (1.58mm) to $3/16''$ (4.76mm) in thickness, with an arbor hole of $1/32''$—0.79mm—(see Fig. 2-18). Incidentally, the $6''$ (152.40mm) silicon carbide wheel is a very helpful intermediary tool. It is usually mounted in the tub-type gem cutting outfit for which it was created (see Fig. 2-19). Its usefulness for gem carving in this setup can be enhanced by raising it on the shaft, thus adding to the clearance between the lower edge of the "lap" (see Glossary) and the bottom of the machine. This can be achieved by mounting two or three flanges or thick metal washers on the shaft below the wheel (see Fig. 2-20).

Making Your Own Grinding Stones

One of these days a benevolent maker of grinding wheels will cover himself with glory by making $3''$ (76.20mm) and $4''$ (101.60mm) grinding wheels in thicknesses of $1/4''$ (6.35mm) to $5/8''$ (15.81mm), with various arbor hole sizes from $1/4''$ (6.35mm) to $1/2''$ (12.70mm), and in the right hardness of bond for lapidary use. In the meantime, this gap may partially be bridged by making one's own grinding stones. To do this, a worn-down $1 1/2''$ (38.10mm) or $2''$ (50.80mm) thick grinding wheel is sawed into slices $3/8''$ (9.52mm) thick, which are then ground on the regular wheels into a round shape (see Fig. 2-21). The slices must be of even thickness. Then, a hole is dug in the center of the disk with nails—square steel nails are also good for this purpose. It may sound like an impossible undertaking, since the grit in the wheel is harder than a nail, and in the ordinary course of things the wheel would grind down the nails. In practice it works, however. What happens is that the nail is harder than the bond which holds the grit. This is chipped away by the sharp edges and irregularities at the point of the nail. Holding the nails which are expected to do the grinding in a "brace and bit," will take some of the fatigue out of this laborious enterprise (see Fig. 2-22). Eventually, the nails are worn smooth and will have to be replaced. They are still usable as nails, however, so that there is no waste.

The improvised grinding disk is then fastened to a mandrel, if one can be found

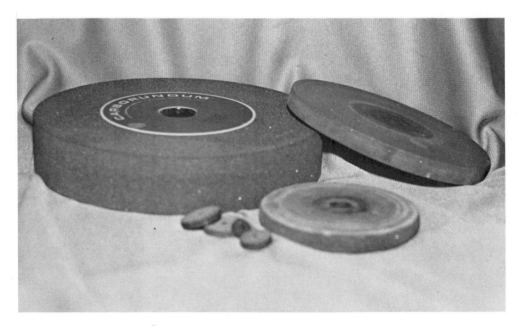

Fig. 2-18 Various size grindstones.

Fig. 2-19 Grindstone mounted in tub type machine.

Fig. 2-20 A washer on spindle below grindstone to add clearance.

Fig. 2-21 Homemade grind-stones made from worn wheels.

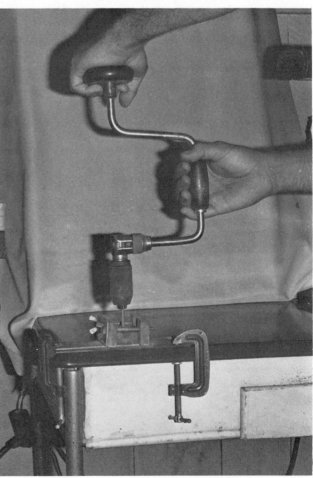

Fig. 2-22 Brace and bit used in making homemade wheels.

which is large enough, or "epoxied" to a nail, the head of which has been sawed off, or glued (with epoxy) to a short length of steel drilling rod not larger than a $1/4"$ (6.35mm) thick. Before fastening shaft to disk, the former should be tested to see that it will run true in the drill. For this test it is inserted into the drill chuck which is then set in motion. If it does not run true, there will be a blur without distinct outline. If the nail or rod just seems to stand still after being switched on, all is well. To make sure that the two constituents of the grinding implement being created are at right angles to each other, the disk should be rested on the drill table and the piece forming the shaft is inserted in the drill chuck until the epoxy sets. There should be a piece of wax paper between disk and table to avoid gluing the two together (see Fig. 2-23).

Since this immobilizes the drill for any other use while the glue is setting, a jig may be used to hold the two pieces to be joined in correct alignment. A very simple version of this can be made by drilling a hole through a thin board, using a drill press or gem drill; the hole being of the exact size of the nail to be used as a shaft. By resting this board on top of a vise (which is usually employed to hold material while it is being drilled), with the nail inserted through it into the grinding stone, correct alignment, sufficient for our purpose, is assured (see Fig. 2-24). If the epoxy method is used, it is not necessary to pierce the hole all the way through, but it should be deep enough to give the glue a good grip. After the epoxy is well set, the disk is trued by holding a piece of the old grinding

Fig. 2-23 Drill is used as jig.

Fig. 2-24 Jig improvised from piece of wood and drill vise.

wheel against it while it is running in the drill. It is good to make several grinders like this and to have them available in two or three different sizes and grits (see Fig. 2-25).

There is a Royal lawn mower sharpener obtainable in many hardware stores to be used on a ¼″ (6.35mm) portable electric drill (see Fig. 2-26). The grindstone, which is 2″ (50.80mm) in diameter, is manufactured with a bond just soft enough for lapidary work. It can be epoxied to a nail just like the homemade disk, but is not quite so effective because it is just a little harder (see Fig. 2-27). For even finer work there are various forms or commercially made grinding bits of silicon carbide on fixed mandrels. These come in sizes ⅛″ (3.17mm) to ¼″ (6.35mm) in diameter, and in different shapes such as disks, cylinders, cones, balls, etc. (see Fig. 2-28). They are fairly expensive because they wear fast and, when used up, have to be discarded, shaft and all. There are, however, certain operations which can only be performed with just such specialized tools. Often these points are only sold in sets. My recommendation is to buy such a set of ten or twelve tools to be prepared for any situation which will arise, and to shop around for a source to replace single points as they are used up.

Fig. 2-25 New and used homemade grindstones.

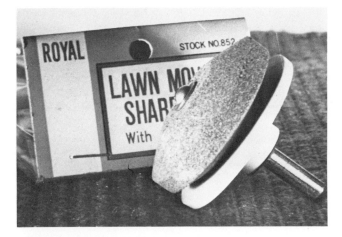

Fig. 2-26 Lawn mower sharpener before conversion.

Fig. 2-27 Lawn mower sharpener made into grindstone for carving.

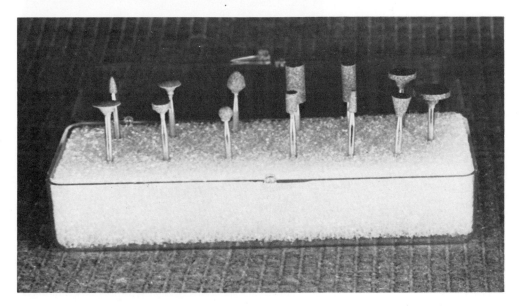

Fig. 2-28 A set of factory-made grinding points.

A more economic operation can be achieved by use of the minute wheels (1"—25.40mm—or less in diameter) which have been mentioned before in passing. The brand I am familiar with, and which, so far as I know, is the only one of its kind available, is called Mizzy Heatless. They are counterparts of the larger wheels we are familiar with, except for size and the bond which is very soft. This makes the little wheels very effective, but they also wear away very fast. They do, indeed, live up to their name, and generate little heat even under prolonged use. The only reason to use water with them is to lay the dust generated by grinding.

This is as good a place as any to remind the reader that there are some potential dangers involved in gem carving. The problem is at its worst when carving for detail with a flexible shaft tool or hand-held electric grinder such as the Dremel. Heretofore it was impossible to keep some of the abraded material, both gemstone powder and particles from the grinding bits, from landing on one's person. This is particularly bad when water has to be used as a coolant. I have come up with a device which will practically eliminate this nuisance.

I built a 1" x 1¹/₂" (25.40mm x 38.10mm) wood frame to support a pane of glass or plastic (Figs. 2-29 and 2-30). The worker sits in front of the device while the project is being handled behind the pane. This then catches all the debris and spray which would otherwise land on the carver's face or, at best, on his clothes. The support of the frame, which rests on the work table, should be big enough to hold a water container in such a way that it is easily removable. The glass or plastic rests loosely on the frame so that the cleaning of it, which has to be done quite frequently, is easy. I used a ¹/₄" (6.35mm) thick, 12" x 12" (304.80mm x 304.80mm) acrylic pane. The frame required two 6' (1.83 meters) pieces of 1" x 1¹/₂" (25.40mm x 38.10mm) lumber.

Now, coming back to the minute wheels, they are made to be mounted on reusable mandrels and come in various thicknesses and diameters, 1" (25.40mm) or less. Since 1" (25.40mm) wheels are sold at the same price as the lesser diameters, it pays to order only the largest size, and, at different stages of wear, save some to be used later as needed.

Fig. 2-29 Front view of the spray catcher.

Fig. 2-30 Side view of the spray catcher. A streak of intercepted debris is visible on the window.

The carver should own the two different thicknesses they come in. Considerable savings are possible by buying them in lots of at least a dozen, with lots of fifty still being cheaper. Since they are consumed at a very fast clip, it is well worthwhile to take advantage of this economy.

Another useful small grinding tool, which is actually a cross between a grinding wheel and a saw, is the cutoff disk (see Fig. 2-31). It comes in one diameter ($7/8''$— 22.22mm) for mounting on a mandrel. It is very delicate and will break fairly easily on being twisted, but cuts very fast. For incising fine lines, it is as good as a diamond tool of the same thickness, but a lot cheaper. In all fairness, it should be said, however, that diamond tools, by offering a great choice of thicknesses and edge shapes, will perform tasks which the cutoff disk cannot do. Mounting two or three of the cutoff disks on a mandrel will give the carver a cutting wheel which will work a bit slower than the Mizzy wheels, but will keep its shape much longer. Here, also, it is recommended to save disks in various stages of wear to be equipped for diverse requirements. There is considerable

Fig. 2-31 Cut-off disks loose and mounted.

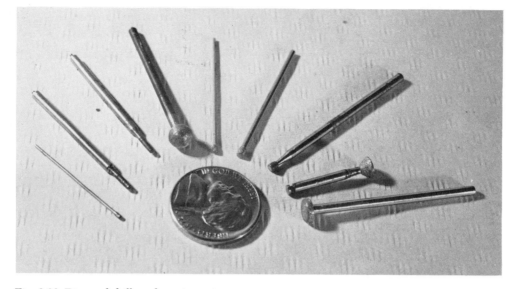

Fig. 2-32 Diamond drills and carving points.

difference in the effectiveness of the disks made by various manufacturers. Some will cut slower and last longer, others will wear away faster but speed up work. I prefer the latter kind. These are grey in color and are marketed by various dental supply firms.

Grinding can also be done with various steel, iron, aluminum, brass, and copper tools, used in conjunction with silicon carbide powders or diamond powders and a lubricant (usually water). In this case, arrangements will have to be made to confine the slurry to the grinding point and to raise and lower the drill at frequent intervals to admit new grit to the working surface. Methods will be studied at length in the chapter on drilling.

Inexpensive silicon carbon points, intended by the manufacturer to be used for working metal on portable electric hand drills, may also be employed to carry a mixture of loose silicon carbide grit and lubricant like the metal points. They come in a wide choice of useful shapes, but, as they are, will not work stone because the bond holding the abrasive is too hard. Also on the market are rubber-bonded silicon carbide points going by the trade name of Cratex. They come in different sizes (up to 2″—50.80mm—in diameter), in three grades (fine, medium, and rough), and in various shapes (disks and several bullet forms). While they do a little cutting, they are principally useful as sanding tools, doing a particularly good job on jade.

Some grinding is also done with diamond tools. The use of the diamond saw to remove material which has been mentioned is, of course, nothing else but employing the saw as a grinding wheel. For fine detail carving, diamond points in various shapes (see Fig. 2-32) are without peers for all materials except, possibly, the cryptocrystalline quartzes. Even for these diamond points may have to be used on occasion, because there is no other tool which will do what they can accomplish. More will be said on diamond tools when discussing their use in drilling.

Water Supply in Carving

Unlike the standard cabochon machinery, none of the units activating the small carving tools have provisions for water supply built in. Water, by the way, is the only practical lubricant for carving because no one has as yet come up with a foolproof solution for avoiding the ubiquitous spray problem. Water can be supplied to the spot where the wheel touches the work in a number of ways. For drilling, it can be confined to a small spot by dams or fences, as we shall see later. For freehand carving, the easiest way is to rig a transfusion bottle—as used in hospitals—to drip in the right spot by attaching it to a strong, but flexible wire. If such a bottle is unobtainable, there is a similar arrangement available commercially. It has been advertised lately in the magazines as "The Little Dripper." In using the Mizzy wheels, theoretically, water is not necessary since the wheels are justly proclaimed as "heatless" by their maker. I like to use the coolant, however, if a great deal of grinding is to be done to lay the dust.

When other silicon carbide wheels are employed and the materials worked on are not too heat sensitive, enough water may be supplied by having a container of it handy to dip the carving and the carving point at short intervals. Do not dip the point while it is running or you will take an unwanted shower. A better way is to hold a wet sponge so that it touches the tool, or preferably, both the tool and the work. The drip method, however, is the best, particularly for diamond points. Incidentally, splashing will be minimized if the water is dripped on the material being carved (not the revolving tool) in such a way that it flows toward the working spot. Since the application of all these tools involves the use of electric motors, care should be taken to keep the splashing water away from them. This is not too much of a problem since, with both the gem drills and flexible shaft tools, the revolving point is some distance away from the power source, and the water thrown would not be directed at the motor. However, it is a point which should be kept in mind continuously.

Drilling

Drilling is a variant of the carving operation which produces round holes or indentations by means of solid metal points or tubing, either in conjunction with loose abrasives, or with diamond powders integrated in the drill. The drill is probably the oldest gem carving instrument used by man and was originally rotated between the palms of both hands. Later it was refined into the bow-drill, a version of which is still used in many places to drill pearls. Today the drill is commonly driven by electric motor.

Drills may be improvised by using point carvers and especially true-running portable electric drills in stands which are sold for this purpose. Usually, such arrangements are not very satisfactory. Regular drill presses may be adapted if the chucks will hold the small tools involved. If any of these improvisations are used with loose grits, arrangements will have to be made to raise and lower the drill or the platform on which the work is mounted, in order to permit fresh grit to fall under the cutting edge of the bit as it rotates. The best instrument, if it can be afforded, is a gem drill specially built for this purpose, as has been mentioned in the chapter on carving. It will raise and lower the drilling point automatically by a cam arrangement. Besides being usable as a carver, it can also be converted to drilling with diamonds or even as a light drill press for work on materials other than gemstones. I have used the Pro-Carva gem drill for a long time and the following descriptions are specifically for this instrument. But as all the drills on the market differ in detail only, it should not be difficult to adapt the instructions to other machines.

The drill, fundamentally, consists of three principal parts (see Fig. 2-33). The most important of these is the drilling rig proper (P). It is supported by the mast and pedestal assembly (A) to which is also attached the drilling platform or table (F).

The drilling rig, in turn, consists of two motors and the drill (G). One of these motors operates the drill by means of a rubber belt. The drill consists of a drill shaft with a pulley on one end, and a Jacob's chuck (H) on the other. It revolves in a bearing (N). The drill unit, bearing and all, is fastened to the rest of the assembly so that it is capable of a limited up and down movement. The other motor operates a cam (O) which, if adjusted to do

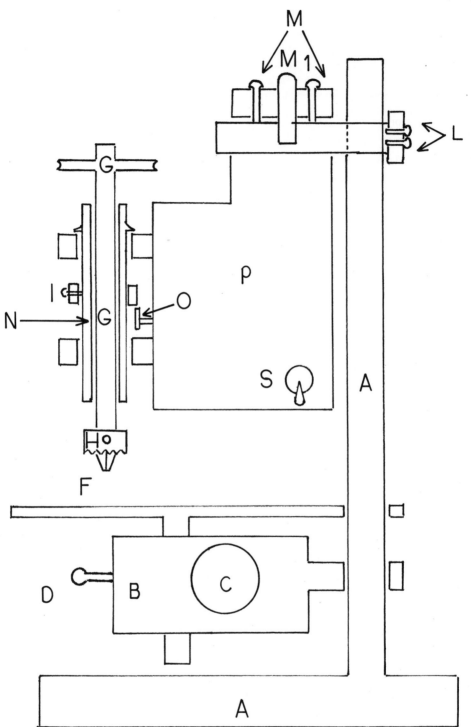

Fig. 2-33 Diagram of the Pro-Carva gem drill.

Fig. 2-34 Chuck-key chained to drill platform.

Fig. 2-35 Two hexagonal screws holding drill assembly to mast.

so, lifts the drill assembly by touching an adjustable collar (I) which is fastened to the bearing. This collar, when raised as far as it will go and fixed at that point, will convert the gem drill into a small drill press. The switch (S), if thrown forward toward the front of the machine, will activate both the motor driving the drill and the one agitating the cam. If turned in the opposite direction, it will only operate the motor driving the drill. The drilling platform assembly is operated by two wheels and a lock screw. One of the wheel handles (to the left facing the machine) permits the platform to be moved up or down, sideways, or out of the way altogether when loosened, and to be fixed into place when tightened (see Fig. 2-34). The other one (C) is used to adjust the height of the table after it has thus been fastened into place. The lock screw (D) will then hold it in that position. The drilling rig can also be raised or lowered by means of the set screws (L) which hold its support to the mast (see Fig. 2-35). When the drill is to be tilted, two screws (M) which secure it to the supporting member, are loosened and a pin (M1) located in the center between them is withdrawn (see Fig. 2-36). The drill is then secured in the desired position by tightening these screws. Later, the drill can be returned to an exactly vertical position by reversing the process and reinserting the pin.

The drill bits which do the actual piercing of the gemstone may be either solid blunt steel points or metal tubing. The solid points could be steel needles with their points broken or ground off, or nails with their heads removed. For example, #12 or #14 brads, $1^1/2''$ (38.10mm) long, with their heads filed or ground down, could be so utilized. Metal tubing is available starting from $1^1/2$mm in diameter to as much as the drill will swing. On the Pro-Carva, 2″ (50.80mm) drills are the largest which can be handled without trouble. The very small sizes up to $5/32''$ (0.025mm) may be inserted full length into the hollow quill of the Pro-Carva so that only as much as is needed for the moment protrudes from the chuck (see Fig. 2-37). Tubes up to $1/4''$ (6.35mm) in diameter can be inserted into the chuck of the drill as they are; larger tubing will have to be fitted to a holder. For holes of $2^1/2$mm or less, both solid and tube drills may be used. For larger holes, solid drills are so inefficient that tube drills are much more preferable. Even for the smaller sizes, the only thing a solid drill has to recommend itself is cost.

Core drills (see Fig. 2-38) may be bought ready-made, or any small diameter metal tubing may be cut up and put to work. Empty ballpoint pen refills, for example, make good drills, but they must be cleaned thoroughly to remove ink residues, which is very messy. Surplus hardware stores often carry small diameter brass and aluminum tubes. The latter are very effective in soft materials such as serpentine. Tubing with very thin walls should have a core inserted in that part which is held in the chuck because, otherwise, it will be deformed and thus thrown off center. The commercially made core drills come in standard lengths of 2″ (50.80mm) for those up to 1″ (25.40mm) in diameter, and in lengths up to 3″ (76.20mm) for those 1¹⁄₈″ (28.57mm) to 3¹⁄₂″ (88.90mm) in diameter. However, longer and shorter drill tubes may be had without difficulties at a nominal charge.

Size 200 silicon carbide grit is commonly used for drilling with metal cores or solid metal points, but finer grades of the abrasive may be employed for holes in transparent material which are intended to be polished on the inside. Drilling with loose grits calls for confining the mixture of lubricant and cutting agent close to the drilling point. Most instructions I have read recommend modeling clay for this, but I've never had satisfactory results with it. For small holes in the sizes of 2mm or thereabouts, a low dam of steel sash putty will do very well. It adheres much better to the material to be drilled than modeling clay. For higher dams, adhesive tape or decorator's tape serves much better. It should be stressed, however, that for all these adhesives the gem material must be bone dry to start with or they will not stick. The tapes may be used by themselves or they can be reinforced.

Many kinds of makeshifts come in handy as stiffeners. A small metal funnel may be cut down. Aluminum from soft drink containers, sections of toothpaste tubes, or frozen juice cans all make good collars to hold the coolant (see Fig. 2-39). The actual drilling procedure is described in great detail in Chapter 5, on snuff bottle carving. References to other varieties of drilling will also be made in Chapters 7, 13, 14, and 15, on the making of beads, ashtrays, pendants, and the manufacture of a cup and saucer.

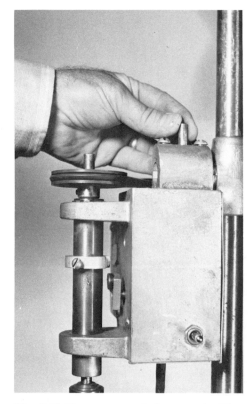

Fig. 2-36 Two screws and plug permit tilting and return to original position of the drill rig.

Fig. 2-37 Twelve-inch-long thin metal tubing used for drilling.

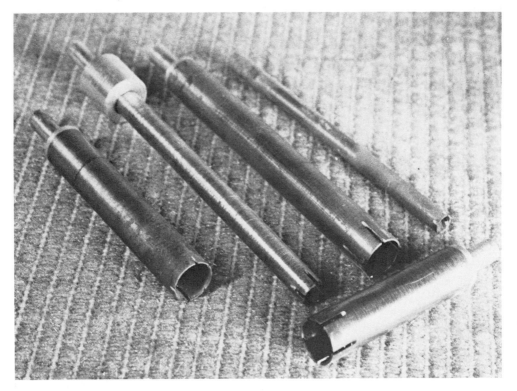

Fig. 2-38 Metal core drills.

Fig. 2-39 Improvised collars to retain coolant.

Diamond Tools

I have saved the discussion on diamond tools to the last because, for lapidaries, their application is of very recent vintage. They were developed for industrial use and as dental tools, and lapidaries were late in recognizing their value. Their main drawback is their initial high purchase price. No one I know has made a study of cost per work unit performed, comparing tools using silicon carbide and similar abrasives with diamond tools, but I believe, from my experience, that diamond tools are a bit more expensive to use. However, the difference in the long run, particularly for the average amateur carver, is small, provided that good quality, well made instruments are employed.

Principally, there are two kinds of diamond tools. In the less expensive ones, diamond is plated onto metal shapes one layer deep. In the more costly ones, a mixture of metal powder and diamond is sintered to a metal core. Reputable dealers will be glad to disclose both the depth of impregnation, and the percentage of diamond to metal. The plated tools have their uses, particularly for those who do very limited drilling, or who work with soft gem materials such as peridot. As a whole, the sintered tools are much to be preferred.

The carver will be concerned mainly with three varieties of diamond charged tools apart from the regular diamond saws. They are solid drills, hollow core drills, and carving points. All of these have certain characteristics in common. They are sensitive to heat and should never be run without sufficient coolant, water being preferable in most cases because of the splash problem. They should revolve at high speeds. On the Pro-Carva drill, they are run at motor speeds of 5000 rpm. Speeds on this drill are changed by replacing the pulley used for ordinary work on the revolving quill with a smaller one of the same size as the one on the motor (see Fig. 2-40 and Fig. 2-41). Diamond tools are

Fig. 2-40 The regular pulley setup on the Pro-Carva.

Fig. 2-41 Small pulley on drill will speed revolutions.

uneconomical for drilling, or carving agates, or other cryptocrystalline quartzes. But even on these, it may be occasionally necessary to employ them for fine detail work which cannot be done any other way.

While there does not appear to be any noticeable difference in time elapsed for drilling holes of a given depth, diamond tools offer a number of advantages over tools using or made of ordinary abrasives. Diamond drills will not be shortened measurably from one hole to the next, which helps greatly in controlling depth of cuts. The coolant (water) is clear enough to permit easy lining up of holes. Holes made with diamond core drills show much less variation from bottom to top than those made with other abrasives. Diamond carving points are available in a much wider choice than those made from silicon carbide, and they will keep their original shape for a long time. If sintered diamond tools seem to stop working, but on inspection are not deformed and have lots of diamond left, they can be "resharpened" by touching them very shortly while running to a piece of grinding stone.

For completeness' sake, I should mention that diamond tools can be made at home. Good instructions for this are given in the book by Forrest W. Pond titled *How To Make and Use Gem Carving Tools* (see Bibliography).

Making diamond tools entails mostly the impregnation of small copper and brass rods and disks with large mesh (80–100) diamond powders. This is done by notching them and then filling the notches with a mixture of diamond and oil or Vaseline, and then hammering them shut. I have tried this. Not only did I follow Mr. Pond's instructions, I also experimented on my own. I substituted a flat piece of agate for the steel anvil Mr. Pond recommends, and another wedge of agate about $1/2''$ (12.70mm) by $3''$ (76.20mm) by $4''$ (101.60mm) for the hammer, finding that the diamond will not imbed itself in the agate as it will in steel. I prepared a small amount of mixture of 100 grit diamond powder and Vaseline to charge my tools. Then, with the compound, I covered a $1/2''$ (12.70mm) brass hinge pin and a small $3/16''$ (4.76mm) bronze bearing (soldered to a nail shaft with silver solder). Using strong pressure, I rolled the diamond compound into the tool heads. When impregnated they look as though they had been well sanded. These tools, as well as the other ones in Mr. Pond's book, do work. But after experimenting with them and comparing them with well made commercial ones, it is easy to understand why no one makes homemade diamond saws any more.

My conclusions are that it is advisable to use diamond points for all drilling of small holes with solid drills and with core drills in all but the cryptocrystalline quartzes up to $1''$ (25.40mm) in diameter. In larger diameters, the purchase price of the points is too high to make sense for the average amateur. For fine detail carving, diamond points are without peers for all materials. There will probably come a time when gem carvers will look back at us with pity for using carving tools other than diamond charged ones, just as we regard the poor benighted ancestors—of so recent vintage that many of us barely missed being counted among them—who used mudsaws or homemade diamond blades for cutting rocks asunder.

Sanding

After all the cutting has been accomplished, the product is sanded. Again, full size sanding equipment is employed as much as possible. Some recesses can be reached by arranging the belt on a sanding drum so that it overhangs a little to one side or the other. This is easiest to do on the type of sanding drum where the belt is held in place by a rubber cushion which expands when in motion. Care should be taken not to touch the very edges of the overhang while the wheel is running, either with the fingers or the gemstone being worked, since they may inflict a painful cut or, what is even worse, the carving may be marked by a gash deep enough to call for regrinding. Much detail sanding may be done on a 6″ (152.40mm) maple disk, run either in a tub-type machine or on the shaft of a carver. For this purpose the wood would be charged with a mixture of silicon carbide with either Carbopol, mineral oil, or water. In such work, the periphery and edges of the lap will do the most useful execution.

There are also miniature sanding drums on the market for which sanding sleeves are sold in most hardware stores. To replace these small belts when they are worn, a screw on top of the holding device is loosened. When the new belt is in place, tightening the screw will hold it securely. These sanders will do some cutting when new, particularly on the softer materials. The sleeves come in rough and fine grit, and they always have to be used dry. As a rule, their top edges get worn out first. To get all possible wear out of them, after a while, it pays to reverse them top to bottom.

Little wooden disks put on the same mandrels as used on the Mizzy grinding disks, charged with the silicon carbide slurry, do much of the sanding in tight places. Wooden buttons or beads, which can be found in all notions stores, fixed to the same mandrels or epoxied to nails, will serve the same purpose (see Fig. 2-42).

Small sanding disks are available in sizes from ¹/₂″ (12.70mm) to 1″ (25.40mm). These are good for sanding in crevices, particularly curved ones. They can be stiffened by mounting them back to back or by underlaying them with disks cut from thin plastic that is found in box covers for candy and stationery. These disks wear out on the edges first, but their life can be prolonged by trimming the used-up part with nail scissors.

Places which cannot be reached otherwise may be sanded by hand using a piece of sanding cloth which is folded either on itself, or over a core of suitable shape. This system works astonishingly well and faster than one would expect. Occasionally, to shorten the time required for sanding, deeper scars in such confined places can be smoothed out by a point cut to suitable shape from a worn-out 600 grit grinding wheel. A strand of picture wire does sanding in holes and other very narrow places. One end of the wire is fastened to a drawer knob or other fixed projection, and the other end is held by hand and charged with slurry. Cratex wheels, which have been mentioned previously, are also fine for sanding.

Fig. 2-42 Wooden beads and buttons made into sanding and polishing tools.

When there is a great deal of sanding to be undertaken at one time, it is best to start with a new sanding cloth and go over the whole figure, or batch of figures as thoroughly as possible. To improve the finish of the first operation, the process is repeated with the same cloth which, by that time, is somewhat worn. A very well worn cloth is resorted to for the final sanding. When sanding for any length of time it is advisable to wear a dust mask.

Polishing

When the carving is well sanded, it may or may not have to be polished. Many carvings, particularly figure carvings, look better in the matte finish imparted by sanding. It is not necessary to impart a mirror polish to a carving just because it is made from gemstone. Sometimes it is advisable to only polish part of a figure or only some highlights. This is a matter for the carver to decide. If he decides to polish, again, as in all previous operations, standard equipment is called on for as much of the work as possible.

Convex leather-covered polishing disks will do the brunt of the polishing job. Even more useful are muslin buffs 6″ (152.40mm) to 8″ (203.20mm) in diameter, and run vertically. Different buffing wheels must, of course, be used for each grit and kept in dust-proof plastic bags when not in use. Soaking these buffs in a water suspension of the specific polishing powder, and permitting them to dry partially before use will result in better performance because less of the polishing medium will be flung off in operation. To keep down heat, they must be kept moist with the addition of water and, occasionally, polishing mixture.

Hard felt wheels—6″ (152.40mm), and 8″ (203.20mm)—also do yeoman service (see Fig. 2-43). They may be run vertically or horizontally in one of the tub-type machines. The latter method requires some sort of support of the disk, which should be somewhat smaller than the felt being supported, to permit the rim and edges of the wheel to come into play. The older these felt buffs grow, the more useful they become for carving because they soften a bit, and thus accommodate themselves more easily to irregular contrours (see Fig. 2-44).

There are small wheels to fit on the miniature mandrels made both of felt and muslin. The same trick mentioned for the larger buffs, of soaking them before use, applies, of course, to these also. Small felt buffs can be punched from old felt hats, using a small diameter pipe sharpened at one rim as a punch. The wooden wheels, beads, and buttons recommended for sanding may also be used for polishing in conjunction with regular polishing powders or, if the occasion warrants, with diamond compounds in the very fine grades.

Very tight places may be reached using points of thin wooden dowels held in the chuck of the carver. These dowels are more apt to run true when they are kept as short as the job will allow.

The trick mentioned before of sanding with picture wire may be adapted for polishing by using cotton string of varying thickness, braided if necessary, and soaked with the polishing mixture.

Round disks, about 6″ (15cm) in diameter and from 1/4″ (6.35mm) to 1/2″ (12.70mm) thick, are sawed from waterproof plywood and drilled in the center with a 1/2″ (12.70mm) arbor hole. Chamois leather (as used for window cleaning) is then stretched over the disk so that the leather lies smoothly on the side which will be used for polishing. The leather is held in place on the other side of the disk using tacks, which are driven through the leather and wood. They are usable for polishing flat, as well as, concave surfaces.

On large flat or slightly curved surfaces, Pellon polishing cloth on a wood or metal

Fig. 2-43 A felt wheel
mounted on motor shaft.

disk support, in conjunction with cerium oxide, will speed and improve the finish of the
quartzes, both crystalline and cryptocrystalline.

Before leaving the subject of the use of carving machinery, I should mention a little
wrinkle which applies to the use of any machine equipped with a Jacob's chuck and,
therefore, also to the drill. This chuck is operated by a key which has a way of hiding or

Fig. 2-44 A well worn felt
wheel is fine for polishing carvings.

being mislaid. To counteract this, I recommend fastening it by a chain equipped with a swivel, as used on basin stoppers, to one of the handles of the drill. It is advisable to establish a routine to remove this key from the chuck as soon as bits are secured. It will otherwise be thrown off violently as soon as the machine is set in motion, which may not only be painful, but also dangerous to the operator.

3
Making a Gemstone Chess Set

To my mind, there is no better project to introduce a newcomer to gem carving than the making of a chess set. At first thought, it may seem an overly ambitious undertaking for an initial attempt at gem sculpture, but it has a number of facts to commend itself for this purpose. Fact one is that while there are 32 pieces to a set, they all can, and for this purpose, should be very simple. Fact two is that each figure has to be repeated at least once, as in the case of the king and queen, and as many as 16 times for the pawns, which makes this project a particularly useful exercise. Fact three is that given a simple enough design, all the work can be performed on the equipment available in any shop set up for cabochon cutting. Fact four is that making the models for the simple shapes involved here is a good and easy introduction to modeling in clay.

The greatest challenge in this project is to think up simple, yet aesthetically satisfying shapes which will fulfill the further requirement of fitting the chessboard for which they are created, without crowding; that they are easily recognizable; and that they have a low center of gravity so they won't topple on slight provocation. Changing the appearance of chessmen from the stereotype format we are used to seeing in most of the sets all over the world may seem a sacrilege to many people. A bit of research will show, however, that the traditional pattern originated because it is easy to manufacture on a wood turning lathe with a little assistance from a whittling knife. It will also be found that there are many examples—both modern and going back to the time when the game was invented— of very simple and very elaborate chess figurines of quite different, nonstandardized appearance.

The shapes pictured here (see Fig. 3-1) are the result of long deliberation and experiments, but are, of course, no ultimate solution. To help others to arrive at their own versions, let me give a short recapitulation of the ideas I finally came up with and how I arrived at them. The castles were the easiest. All that was wanted in this case was the depiction of a medieval keep in its most primitive form. I thought about crenellating the top of the towers by saw cuts, but decided against it because I thought it would look too busy, so the figures are tapered ever so slightly toward the top.

46

Fig. 3-1 Clay models for chessmen: Left to right, bishop, castle, king, queen, knight, and pawn.

The pawns also presented no problems. I first considered making them cylindrical with half globes for tops, and then making them into cubes, but ended up with oblong shapes, square in the cross section and terminating at the upper end into a flat pyramid.

The bishops gave me a hard time until I hit on the thought of representing them by a stylized version of a bishop's mitre. A saw cut incision separates the front and back parts, which are identical.

The queen is depicted in flowing robes and head dress, very simple and severe, as befits a queen in war time (chess, as we should not forget, is a war game).

The king also is dressed in a flowing mantle, narrowing a little towards his feet. He is portrayed wide-shouldered and deep-chested, wearing a visored helmet, which originally was oval in the cross section, but was changed in the finished version to a diamond shape because I thought it looked better.

The knight was the figure most difficult to arrive at. While I was sure that I wanted a horse's head, it was hard for me to figure out a simple enough, yet clearly recognizable shape. The final form is the result of countless doodles and experiments in clay. Since it is a rather complicated figure, it is difficult to describe in words, and the pictures will have to speak for themselves.

The first step in actually creating the set is to choose a board on which it will be displayed, as this will determine the size of the individual pieces. I selected a board, the fields of which are 2″ (50.80mm) square. This is slightly larger than the common run of chess sets, but not so unusual that it would be hard to find.

Next, Plasticine models are made of each of the 16 pieces needed for one side: the king, the queen, two castles, two bishops, two knights, and eight pawns. These should be done in the exact size in which they will be translated into gemstone. They are then displayed on the board for looks and size.

Next comes the procurement of suitable material. To find out what is needed, we have to ascertain the maximum dimensions of the clay models, and order for each a rectangular block containing these measurements. The sizes given in the following table are those I arrived at for the set here described, which, I repeat, are changeable at will for different designs and sizes, and are as follows:

Chess piece	Dimensions in inches (mm.)	No. of pieces needed	Total amount needed
Pawns	1½ x ⅞ x ⅞ (38.10 x 22.22 x 22.22)	8	1½ x 2 x 4¼ (38.10 x 50.80 x 107.95)
King	2¾ x 1¼ x 1 (69.85 x 31.75 x 25.40)	1	2¾ x 2½ x 1½ (69.85 x 63.50 x 38.10)
Queen	2¾ x 1½ x 1¼ (69.85 x 38.10 x 31.75)	1	2¾ x 2½ x 1½ (69.85 x 63.50 x 38.10)
Knights	2¼ x 2 x 1 (57.15 x 50.80 x 25.40)	2	2¼ x 2¼ x 2 (57.15 x 57.15 x 50.80)
Bishops	2¼ x 1¼ x 1 (57.15 x 31.75 x 25.40)	2	2¼ x 2¼ x 1¼ (57.15 x 57.10 x 31.75)
Castles	2¼ x 1 x 1 (57.15 x 25.40 x 25.40)	2	2¼ x 2¼ x 1 (57.15 x 57.15 x 25.40)

Since it will be impossible to find a dealer willing to supply thirty-two, or as few as six blanks cut to exact size, it will be necessary to use a little arithmetic to arrive at the correct size of one or more blocks of material from which the various blanks will be cut. For example, one block 5″ (127mm) long, 3¼″ (78.55mm) wide, and 1½″ (38.10mm) thick, could yield king, queen, and eight pawns; and another block 4½″ (114.30mm) by 4½″ (114.30mm), and 1″ (25.40mm) thick, would provide the material for the remaining figures. (See also Fig. 3-2 for alternate possibilities.) It is advisable to order some spare material to allow for the possibility of faults in the stone which may show up either in the sawing or carving process. Also, some allowance has to be made for mistakes of the carver. Unused material can always be turned into another project.

Everything said in the general discussion on gem material suitable for carving also

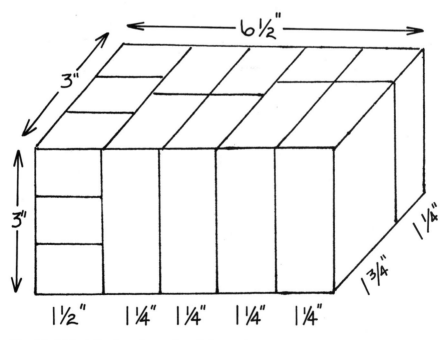

Fig. 3-2 A block lined up for sawing of chess set.

Five snuff bottles (clockwise from left):
tigereye, malachite, sodalite, unakite, rhodonite.

A bear
of Wisconsin jade.

A jade bracelet and two jade rings.

A jade squirrel.

Two spheres (left to right: snowflake obsidian and rhodonite).

Four ashtrays. Top, rhodonite; bottom, left to right, unakite, bloodstone, jade.

Intarsia picture of landscape.

A jade necklace.

A jade cup and saucer.

Chess set
of epidote
and serpentine.

Three epidote
chessmen.

Two jade pendants.

A unakite duck.

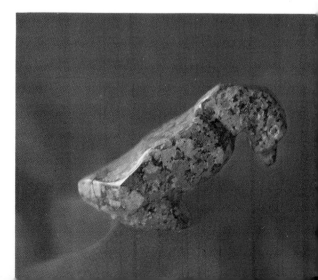

applies, of course, in the making of a chess set, with the added consideration that chess figures are handled more frequently than the average carving and should, therefore, be made from the toughest stone that can be found. The ideal material, as for most carving projects, would be nephrite jade, but it is hard to find jade in colors of sufficient contrast. Massive epidote, serpentine, or rhodonite may be used to good advantage. Jasper and chalcedony are second choices since they chip more readily than the materials named. They are also, of course, a little harder and, therefore, slower to work.

Once the material is in hand, the next step is the sawing of the blanks. This may be done on a trimsaw with a blade 8″ (203.20mm) in diameter or bigger (the larger, the better). Sawing has been discussed at length so that it is not necessary to go into it again here, except to say that in this process of shaping with the saw, it will, of course, save gemstone and time to make the cuts as close to the wanted dimensions as possible. But, if the carver has not had extensive experience in sawing, it might be better to allow for a greater margin of safety. This should be included in the calculations when making out the order for the rough material. All the blanks for both colors of the set should be sawed before going on to the next operation to ensure that suitable and sufficient material is on hand. It is advisable to cut all the pawns from one strip of material. Using the technique of counting revolutions will have them come out practically uniform.

Once the blanks are in hand, individual shaping begins. The first to be cut are the kings and queens since they are the tallest figures. Should it be necessary to diminish their size because of chipping or previously undiscovered flaws, all the other pieces will have to be scaled down if no spare material is on hand. Traditionally, the king is just a hair taller than the queen, but in these days of "Women's Lib," it might be as well to represent both of equal height. White and black kings should be done practically simultaneously. (This applies to the rest of the set as well.) Assuming that we started with a rectangular block, 1¼″ (31.75mm) wide, 1″ (25.40mm) deep, and 2¾″ (69.85mm) high, the next operation would be to make two saw cuts on the trimsaw; one to the right, and one to the left of where the head is going to be. The inside line of the saw kerf should be ⁵⁄₁₆″ (7.93mm) from the outside of the blank, leaving the material from which the head is going to be formed ⁵⁄₈″ (15.87mm) wide (see Fig. 3-3). The cuts should be ⁵⁄₈″ (15.87mm) deep.

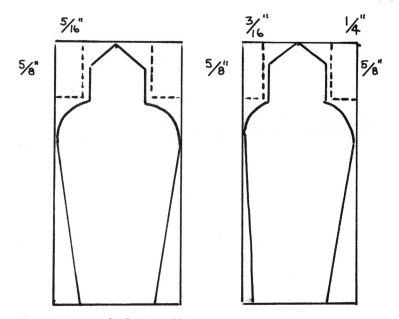

Fig. 3-3 Front and side view of king.

As has been mentioned before, care must be taken to keep the depth of these cuts uniform. The small pieces of waste to the right and left of the head are then sawed off at the appropriate depth by turning the blank 90 degrees. These, and most saw cuts mentioned in the following description of procedures may be omitted if the carver has qualms about using the saw at such close quarters. Unless the material used is very hard and very expensive, it may be easier to grind it away. But, while caution may be the better part of valor, I strongly advocate taking calculated risks rather than the easy way out in order to get familiar with the saw as a tool in gem carving—it will be of unestimable value in the carver's career.

This is as good a place as any to repeat that the saw is a rather delicate instrument. It will be absolutely ruined if its rim is twisted out of shape, and it will not be much good if its set is worn off. All material should, therefore, be either clamped securely, or, if held by hand, should have a level surface of sufficient size to rest on the saw table so it will not wobble while being cut.

After the saw has done its work, the rest of the figure is shaped by grinding. As the carving proceeds, compare the product frequently with the clay model. A special thickness gauge would be the proper instrument, but in its absence, a millimeter gauge or even a small C-clamp may serve (see Fig. 3-4).

When the figure has reached the final stage, finish it off on the finest grinding wheel available, touching very lightly. Some use may be made of the side of the grinding wheel, and, in general, every effort should be made to leave as neat a surface all over the object as humanly possible (see Fig. 3-5). Sanding and polishing should be left to the time when all the set has been ground.

The queen is treated very similarly. For her the size of the blank is $2^3/4''$ (69.85mm) by $1^1/2''$ (38.10mm) by $1^1/4''$ (31.75mm). The cuts next to the head are $1/2''$ (12.70mm) wide, including the saw kerf, $1/2''$ (12.70mm) deep (see Fig. 3-6). Since the front of the figure slants backwards a little, some grinding time and material may be saved by a saw cut starting at the top about $1/4''$ (6.35mm) from, and nearly parallel to, the front of the figure, and ending about $1/2''$ (12.70mm) above the base.

The next figures to be tackled are the knights. Because they are the most elaborate of the lot, as they are being created there is a greater likelihood that mishaps might happen to them than to the rest of the set. This may make it necessary to reduce them in size

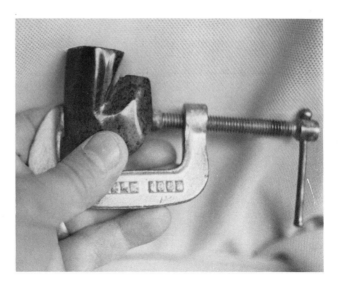

Fig. 3-4 A C-clamp used as a gauge.

Fig. 3-5 The king, carved and polished.

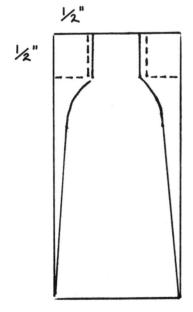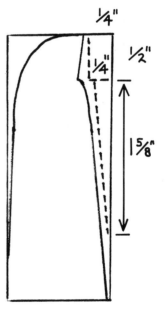

Fig. 3-6 Front and side view of queen.

Fig. 3-7 The queen, carved
and polished.

which would bring about a diminution of the rest of the officers to keep them in propor-
tion, as has been pointed out before.

The blanks for the knights should be 2″ (50.80mm) by 2¹/₄″ (57.15mm) by 1″
(25.40mm). Four saw cuts are called for. Two of these remove small triangular wedges
from the top of the blank (see Fig 3-8). The third is a slanting cut which delineates the
separation of the lower part of the head from the neckline. It starts on a line ¹/₂″
(12.70mm) from the front edge of the base and extends to about the center of the blank. A
fourth cut leads toward this cut, starting about ¹/₂″ (12.70mm) up from the base and parallel to it. Four other saw cuts removing small wedges from the long corners will save a
little time, but are not essential. The edge of the grinding wheel is used to achieve the indentation around and between the ears, the tapering cut to shape the front part of the
neckline, and the underside of the head next to it (see Fig. 3-9). The cutting is done with
the edge of the wheel, slanting to the periphery or to the side of the wheel as circumstances require. This is a departure from common cabochon usage, but with a little practice will not present any difficulties, even to a cutter of only moderate experience.
Frequent inspection of the work will help.

The idea should be kept in mind, however, that the cut will eventually have to be
sanded and polished (see Fig. 3-10). This means that it should be kept as smooth as possible, and not made deeper than necessary, to achieve a satisfactory design. The edge of
the wheel will of course be rounded somewhat by such usage. As has been mentioned in
the general discussion on grinding, this rounding may be brought about on purpose in future projects, but so little of it occurs in this operation that it will disappear in subsequent
grinding.

All four knights should be done in succession. Mishaps, or ideas for the improvement
of the design, made possible by the experience gained in repetition, may occasionally

Side View

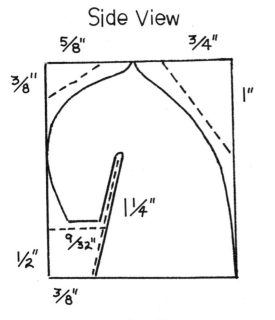

Bottom View

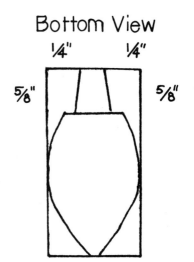

Fig. 3-8 The knight, side and bottom view.

Fig. 3-9 Bottom view of the knight.

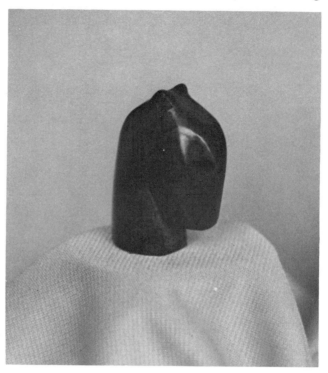

Fig. 3-10 The knight, carved
and polished.

make it necessary or desirable to go back to work on pieces which were previously considered to be finished.

The next pieces to be undertaken are the bishops. They require blanks 1¼″
(31.75mm) wide, 1″ (25.40mm) deep, and 2¼″ (57.15mm) high. After giving each blank
its initial shaping (see Fig. 3-11) an outline of the mitre is drawn on its front and back,
preferably using a template. The blank is then ground to these outlines, making sure that

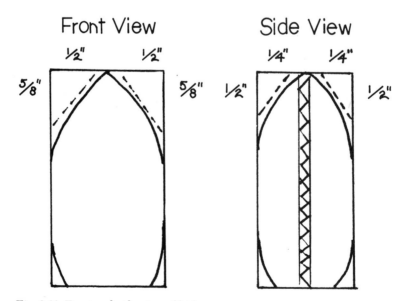

Fig. 3-11 Front and side view of bishop.

Fig. 3-12 Side view of bishop.

the sides are kept even and at right angles to the mitre shaped surfaces. When this has been accomplished, a line is drawn exactly down their center. A saw cut is then made following these lines about ¹/₁₆″ (1.58mm) deep at the base and gradually increasing in depth to as much as ³/₁₆″ (4.76mm) at the point of the figure (see Fig. 3-12). This cut can be made by holding the preform by hand or on a very simple little jig consisting of two small pieces of wood joined in their center by a nail which permits them to rotate. The blank is fastened with dopping cement to one of these, the other piece is held in the saw vise. Either a trimsaw, or an overhead saw may be used. At first, only a very shallow cut is taken, starting at the base and turning the blank very slowly. Once a line has been established, it is fairly easy to stay in the groove. Deepen it gradually by going over it repeatedly until the desired depth is reached. After this, the operation calls for the creation of just two cabochons, back to back, of a truncated pear shape (see Fig. 3-13). If, by bad chance, the saw cuts have been placed a little off center, corrections can be made in the grinding operation. Misplaced saw scratches also may be removed at this stage. The base should be an oval, 1″ (25.40mm) long, and ³/₄″ (19.05mm) wide.

From here on the work is fairly easy. The castles are formed from blanks perfectly square with the base 1″ (25.40mm) on edge. The height should be 2¹/₄″ (57.15mm). The figure should taper to a flat top ⁷/₈″ (22.22mm) square (see Fig. 3-14).

The pawns are ⁵/₈″ (15.87mm) square, and from 1³/₈″ (34.92mm) to 1¹/₂″ (38.10mm) high. They are straight sided. Tops may be left flat or ground into low pyramids if the carver feels ambitious. Grinding these four little triangles on each pawn will be the last major hurdle to overcome (see Fig. 3-15). The glow created by setting up these pieces on the board in their unsanded and unpolished stage should be enough to carry the carver through the rest of the operations.

The first of these is sanding, which can be done by the same procedures as used in

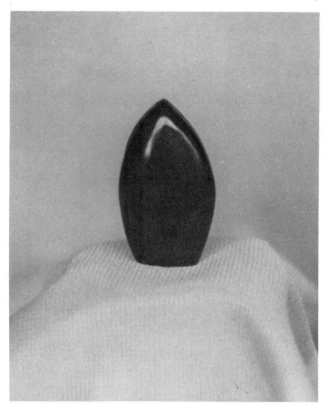

Fig. 3-13 Front view of finished bishop.

Fig. 3-14 Castle and pawn.

Fig. 3-15 Top view of pawn.

cabochon work. To get into some problem areas, such as the neck recesses of the knight, it will be necessary to let the sanding cloth overhang on one edge of the sanding drum. Since there is a great deal of sanding to be undertaken at one time, a new sanding cloth should be used to go over the whole batch. The process is thereafter repeated with the same cloth which, by then, is well worn. Further improvement may be obtained by sanding on a wooden lap with a water or Carbopol suspension of 600 grit silicon carbide. The edge of this disk also will get into some nooks and corners which are not accessible otherwise.

Polishing is accomplished in the same manner as for cabochons. A hard leather lap on wood or metal support is particularly good for jade with either chrome oxide alone, or with a mixture of chrome and Linde A. A felt lap, particularly one that is well worn and, therefore, soft, has surprisingly good results sometimes. This may be run either vertically, or horizontally. Pellon disks are indicated to polish flat or nearly flat surfaces, such as the sides of the castles or pawns.

In carving, even more than in regular cabochon work, it is important to carry each operation to its final stage. It is better to backtrack one step, than to try and sand out a spot which should have been ground out, or to polish out scratches which should have been removed by sanding.

Where some areas cannot be reached by machinery, hand work should be resorted to. A sliver sawed off an old 600 grit grinding wheel, wielded by hand, will eliminate small irregularities in less time than one would expect. A piece of sanding cloth folded on itself or backed by an odd shaped piece of wood or a dowel, as the occasion may require, will work equally well and relatively fast to smooth hard-to get-to places. And finally, a strip of soft leather, clamped on one side to a stationary object, and held by hand on the other, will, in conjunction with the usual polishing compounds, shine up areas other methods cannot reach.

The new sculptor is now ready to challenge Bobby Fisher to a competition in making chess sets out of gem materials.

4
Gem Intarsia Work

A gem intarsia is a picture, all the elements of which are made of gemstone. To fashion one of these in its simplest form furnishes valuable practice for the budding carver both in simplifying a design and in accuracy of grinding.

The project here is a simple landscape, but a flower, or assembly of flowers, or just any uncluttered design might have been chosen. The ordinary practice in making an intarsia is to assemble the pieces after they have been properly shaped; apply them to a background with adhesive such as mastic, epoxy, or anything else which will make them stick; then grind the assembly flat; sand and polish, if desired. This calls for slabs of even thickness as otherwise an inordinate amount of flat lapping has to be done.

We are going to follow a different, somewhat simpler method. This calls for cutting, sanding, and, if necessary, polishing the design elements, assembling them upside down on a flat surface such as a plate of glass, and then only applying the adhesive and backing to the project. The pieces of the intarsia, according to this method, will not have to be of even thickness. By putting them down on the glass, the surface of the picture will be flat. The adhesive on the back of the stone (between stone and backing) will compensate for any unevenness.

The first step is the drawing of the design. It should be kept as simple as possible. Inside curves, particularly deep ones, should be kept to a minimum. The fact that it is easier to fit together two short lines than two long ones should always be kept in mind. Available and purchasable gem material in suitable sizes and colors must also be taken into careful consideration. When the design has been decided on, about half a dozen copies of the original drawing should be made. On one of these, a mirror image of the original is created by holding it up to a window and tracing the outlines visible through the paper. Another one of the copies is numbered in consecutive figures, one number to each element of design (see Fig. 4-1). This is used for reference in the ensuing work. A third copy is then cut up along the lines of the drawing into pieces which will serve as patterns for the gemstone segments to be produced. These paper sections are best kept in order

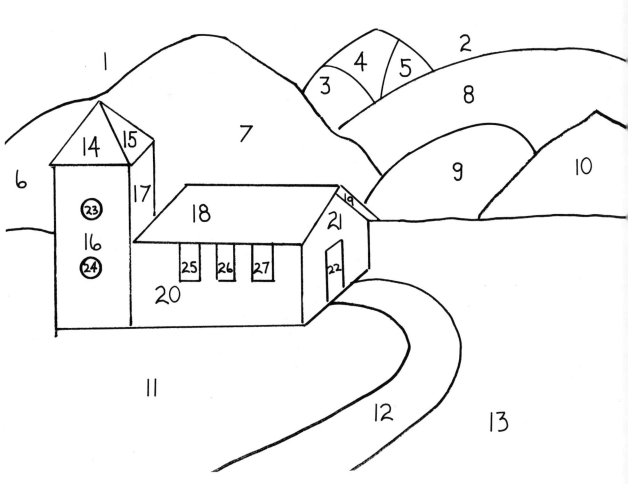

Fig. 4-1 Layout of intarsia project.

until used by sticking them to a transparent sheet of plastic or glass, underlaid with one of the spare copies (with double stick tape) so that they form the picture about to be produced. All these pieces are then numbered in the same way as the reference copy. Then, slabs of material are assembled (see Fig. 4-2).

In the landscape discussed here, serpentine, jade, epidote, agate, Chilean lapis lazuli, rhodonite, and smoky quartz were used. It will simplify matters if the slabs are approximately of the same thickness, but this is not absolutely necessary. There should be sufficient contrast in color to call attention to the central theme (the church in our case). In this picture a variety of greens is needed to make the hills in the background appear to be at varying distances. Since most of the slabs used will not be highly polished, this is a good place to employ materials which have good color and patterns, but which undercut and are otherwise hard to handle.

The paper shapes are now superimposed on the appropriate slabs, and outlined with a black indelible ink marking pen. With saw and grinding wheel, they are then shaped roughly and lined up to check whether they are all present and accounted for. This is also a good time to check whether the whole assembly is satisfactory to look at, as at this stage changes are still easy. Each piece is then marked with the number it has on the drawing which serves as reference (see Fig. 4-3). The numbered side is the one which will show in the finished picture.

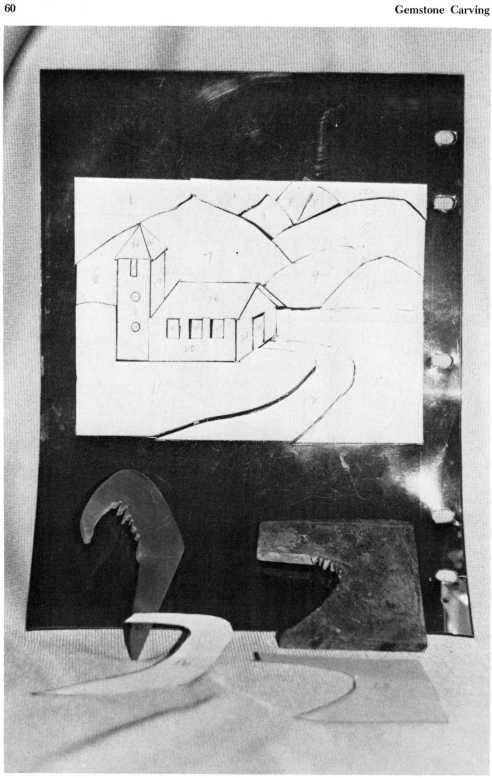

Fig. 4-2 Layout, cut up, and two pieces roughly shaped.

Fig. 4-3 Roughed out pieces assembled and numbered—frame with glass in background.

For the final assembly a frame is made with an opening just large enough to contain the projected intarsia. Wooden lath, which is used in wall construction as a base for plaster and which can be found wherever lumber is sold, is a good material for the frame. It can be glued together, reinforcing the corners with short pieces of the same material. Lath, $1/4''$ (6.35mm) thick, and $1''$ (25.40mm) wide, was used for the frame pictured here. Sections of plywood of suitable thickness could also be used. The wood of this frame should be just a little thicker than the thickest of the slabs to be used. One opening of this frame is covered by a piece of glass which is secured to the wood with decorator's tape. The reverse picture is fastened to the outside of this glass so that it is fully visible when looking through the frame. The gemstone "picture puzzle" pieces are then fitted on the inside of the frame so that they cover the area they are made for. Theoretically, the start for the final fitting together may be made any place, but beginning at the bottom and working up from there, is a logical way to proceed, particularly as the bottom pieces are the largest and most difficult to fit in this case. The reverse picture on the outside of the glass is now not needed any more and is removed.

Most of the grinding for the final fitting can be done on the large wheels which should be well dressed for this purpose. The unavoidable inside curves are preshaped by saw incisions and refined with small wheels either of the homemade kind, or with Mizzy wheels. These are run on a carving machine or a flexible shaft tool.

The cuts should slant slightly so that the surface of the pieces which bear the numbers are ever so slightly larger than the inside surfaces which eventually will be invisible. The idea behind this is to establish a good fit on the visible side, and to form a small V-groove for the adhesive when it is applied. The cutting should be done very cautiously and in small steps. Continuous checking while holding the frame to the light, with the already fitted pieces in place, will disclose high spots which must be ground off to permit a snug fit. This is a complicated game as even a slight move of each segment will affect its relations to all the pieces adjacent to it. It should always be borne in mind that it is the "glass side" which matters most. Only very little grinding will sometimes be needed, and it is easy to overcut. This would then make it necessary to recut a shape entirely. I have found it best to do the final adjustments on a flexible shaft tool with small wheels. Once adjoining pieces have been fitted, they should be affixed to their proper place with double stick tape. This will avoid shifting as others are given their final form, and are then fastened down as well.

After everything is cut and in place, the whole intarsia is removed piece by piece and sanded on the surface which will show. The only pieces polished in this instance were the windows and the door of the church. Pellon was used for this purpose on the smoky quartz from which they were cut. The openings for the square windows were sawed on a trimsaw and touched up with Mizzy wheels run on a flexible shaft tool. The round apertures for the tower windows were made with diamond drills after dopping the blank to a small piece of wood, and surrounding it with a fence of decorator's tape to retain the cooling water. Both in the sawing and drilling, the side which was to be visible was kept uppermost. Both the sawing and drilling were done before the final sanding.

A thin sheet of plastic (Saran Wrap or one of its competitors) is then spread over the inside of the frame—both the wooden parts and the glass. Double stick tape may be used to hold it in place. It is smoothed down well and the picture is laid on top of it, sanded side down. This will keep any adhesive, which might seep through between component parts, from fastening gemstone to glass. If some of the Saran Wrap sticks to the picture, it can be scraped off easily.

Before the final assembly, all the components should be washed (using a brush) with soap and water, rinsed in alcohol, and dried with clean paper towels. The side which will be in contact with the adhesive should not be touched anymore with the fingers.

Everything is then wedged into place, using strips of leather, wood, cardboard, or any combination of these, between the gemstone and the frame. The wedges should be flush with the rest of the picture. Then, a piece of wood, preferably waterproof plywood, the size of the intarsia or slightly larger, is charged with tile cement, which can be purchased at large hardware stores, building supply places, or mail order houses. A last check is made to see that all pieces are properly in place and fitting snugly. The board, thickly covered with adhesive, is then put down on the back of the gemstone so that all of it is in firm contact. Only straight down pressure should be used so that none of the sections of the intarsia will be dislodged. Some of the adhesive may ooze out at the sides and will have to be trimmed off after it hardens. Several days should be allowed for the adhesive to cure as it is slow setting. After the piece is turned right side up, there is the possibility that small gaps will be visible between some components of the picture. These can be filled in with epoxy which is dripped into the openings with a fine wire needle or pin.

An interesting version of this work would be the making of a picture in low relief. It would have to be composed right side up. The pieces would therefore have to be of the right thickness or else they would have to be underlaid with thin layers of metal, wood or cardboard.

5
Making A Snuff Bottle

Snuff bottles are much in vogue these days, not as utilitarian articles, but as decorative objects. Snuff bottles are a Chinese invention. Europeans usually carried their snuff in small boxes called "tabatières," many of which were very ornate. While some were, of course, simple enough, made of horn and wood, there were others of gold, silver, and tortoise shell sometimes set with precious stones and diamonds or else heavily enameled. Contrary to popular belief, there are no really ancient snuff bottles since the habit of taking snuff was introduced into China by way of Europe where, in turn, it had been brought from the Americas. The oldest Chinese snuff bottle is probably not much more than 250 years old. The Chinese snuff bottles are most likely adaptations from perfume bottles which have, of course, a much longer history.

Snuff bottles in their simpler forms are relatively easy to make. The first requirement is a piece of good material. A block of jade 1³/₄″ (44.45mm) wide, 1¹/₄″ (31.75mm) thick, and 2¹/₄″ (57.15mm) or 2¹/₂″ (63.50mm) high, is suggested as a starter. It should be free of cracks and major blemishes, but preferably should not be too expensive. Jade is recommended because it is tough, thus will not be apt to splinter. It will grind somewhat easier than the agates, jaspers, and chalcedonies, particularly in the hollowing-out process. It has the added advantage that many sellers offer it in presawed blocks. Inexpensive material is recommended because it would be a shame to spoil a valuable piece of stone by the mistakes which are likely to occur in a first attempt. It would be just as regrettable to waste a lot of work on a blank which is junk to begin with. I figure that chances of success are three to one or better, so let your purse strings be your guide. After nephrite jade, the next best choices are rhodonite, the better grades of unakite, serpentine, and the cryptocrystalline quartzes, in that order. After the neophyte snuff bottle manufacturer has had more experience, he will be ready to try his hand and drill on such widely available, but more brittle materials as malachite, obsidian, rose quartz, tigereye, sodalite, and aventurine.

Having chosen the material, the next step is to determine the shape of the bottle-to-

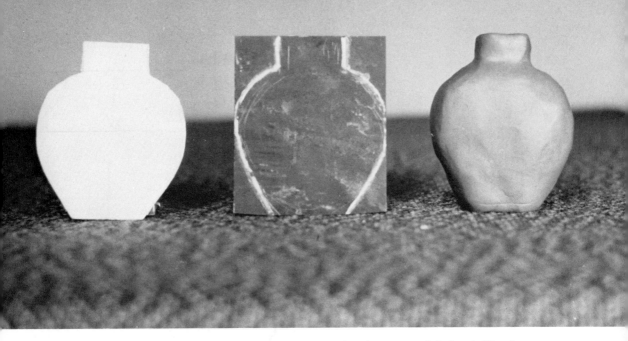

Fig. 5-1 A paper pattern, a block of rough with outline, and a Plasticine model of a snuff bottle.

be. For this purpose, a model is made of clay or Plasticine, based on the material to be worked. Once this is done, an outline of this model is drawn on a piece of strong paper. Then the paper is folded lengthwise in such a manner as to divide the drawing in half. Invariably, one side will be more pleasing than the other. Occasionally part of one outline can be combined to advantage with part of the other. The paper is then cut, still folded, to the chosen design. On unfolding it will present a perfectly symmetrical pattern. This pattern is then traced on the blank with an aluminum pencil or else glued to it (see Fig. 5-1). In the latter case it is a good idea to make a duplicate of the pattern before affixing it to the material. In either case, it is recommended to protect the outline against washing off with acrylic spray or by painting it with clear shellac. After this, a small piece of adhesive tape, about ¼" (6.35mm) square, is applied to the approximate center of the top surface of the material. Using calipers, the exact center is determined and marked on the adhesive tape. A circle slightly larger than the intended hole is then drawn around this spot (see Fig. 5-2). This will probably have to be done first with pencil and redrawn with either an aluminum marker, or indelible ink. The dot of tape will keep the point of the compass from sliding.

We are now ready to drill a hole. For this we need a drilling setup. Drills have been discussed in general in the chapter on equipment, so only the special requirements applying to snuff bottle work will have to be explained here. One of these is that a gap of at least 6" (152.40mm) exists between the lowest point of the drill chuck and the drill platform. A somewhat wider gap will be necessary at times. The distance required depends on the length of the drill bit, which may be 3" (76.20mm) long or more, and the size of the material which could be 3" (76.20mm) high or higher.

To meet this requirement, the makers of the drill furnish a mast 24" (609.60mm) high to replace the standard size one at a nominal charge. I also acquired from them a specially made vise a bit sturdier than the one which comes with the drill as standard equipment (see Fig. 5-3).

It is, of course, possible to attach the blank of gemstone to be drilled, using dopping cement, to a piece of board or plexiglass, which can then be fastened to the drill platform

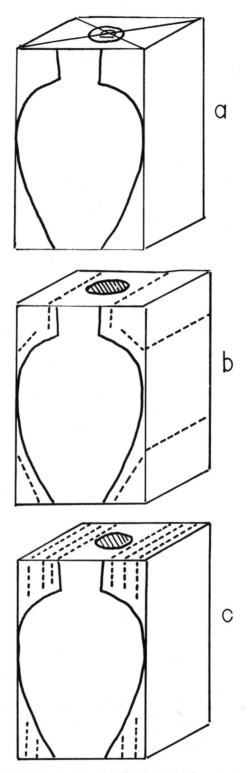

Fig. 5-2 Layout with drill hole and sawcuts indicated: a) applying tape and finding center for
drilling the hole; b) making slanting cuts with
the saw; c) making parallel cuts and breaking off
the resulting piece with a chisel or screwdriver.

Fig. 5-3 Made-to-order drill vises.

with C-clamps. Occasionally, I had bad experiences with this procedure, as at times the steady pounding of the drill loosened the hold of the wax thus creating considerable complications.

Since the drilling in this project will be done with loose grit, abrasive powders in the sizes of 100, 220, and 600 mesh are next required. The finer the grit, the smoother will be the hole, and conversely, the rougher the grit, the faster the drill will work. Smoothness is only important if the bottle is of transparent or very translucent material, in which case the interior of the cut has to be polished. Quart Mason jars with waterproof labels appropriately marked, are good containers for the grits. Each jar should contain one small plastic spoon to feed the abrasive to the work. Also on hand should be a roll of 1½" (38.10mm) adhesive or decorator's tape, an assortment of collars, and a few C-clamps. A bright light just above the working place which can be raised and lowered is a great help. If this cannot be conveniently arranged, a flashlight will do. A couple of eye droppers will round out the list of items required. One of these is kept clean to add water to the work, the other is used to remove surplus grit mixture when indicated.

Next, the block of rough is clamped into the holding device, taking particular care to see that the bottom of the material is exactly flush or parallel to the bottom of the vise (see Fig. 5-4). The assembly is then put on the drill platform, roughly centered, and lightly clamped in place. A drill tube of ½" (12.70mm) outer diameter, 3" (76.20mm) long, is fastened into the Jacob's chuck. Then the drill platform is set at its lowest point. The drilling assembly is adjusted on the mast so that with the drill bit resting on the work

Fig. 5-4 Jade held in vise.

(see Fig. 5-5), the drill is elevated about $^3/8''$ (9.52mm). The block is then exactly centered. Since the circle on top of the jade has been drawn slightly larger than the circumference of the drill bit, this should be easy (see Fig. 5-6). The vise is clamped into place with two C-clamps. They are tightened alternately by degrees, checking continuously to maintain the exact position of the work.

Now a collar of adhesive is constructed. About $^1/2''$ (12.70mm) of this should stick to the material to be hollowed (see Fig. 5-7). The collar may be reinforced with a rim of aluminum cut from a soft drink can, or tin, or lead from a toothpaste tube, or whatever is handy (see Fig. 5-8). The connection of tape to block and tape to tape must be absolutely tight.

A last check is made, with the collar in place, to be sure that the work is correctly centered. Here is where a spot light, or, in its absence, a flashlight is needed. A last minute review is made to see that the clamps are tight and the key of the Jacob's chuck is removed. Then a half teaspoon of 100 grit is inserted in the hollow formed by the collar and water is added, using a squeeze bottle or an eye dropper, to form an emulsion about the thickness of light cream. It pays to be conservative in preparing this mixture, as it is easy to add more, but disconcerting if the drill, on being started, throws water and grit all over.

When all this is accomplished, the switch is thrown in the direction of the operator (standing in front of the drill). This is probably the spot to mention that on the Pro-Carva drill the switch may be moved in two directions. If thrown as indicated, it will activate both the cam motor and the drill. If pushed in the opposite direction, it starts only the drill. If all is well, a whirring sound is heard, interrupted every few seconds by a thump as the cam lifts the drill to permit abrasive to fall under the drill bit. If the thump is not heard, the drill should be shut off and the ring with setscrew (see Fig. 5-9) which surrounds the bearing of the drill adjusted (see Fig. 5-10), so that it will lightly engage the cam (see Fig. 5-11).

A very small touch is all that is required at the start because the contact gets longer as the drill sinks into the work. It can now, theoretically, be left alone until the bit chews all the way down from the $^3/8''$ (9.52mm) height it was elevated to, to begin with. Practically, it is a good idea to stand by every few minutes to check, with the flashlight if necessary, that the collar of adhesive is watertight, and that the right mixture of abrasive and water is maintained. Should a leak develop at this early stage, it would probably be best to remove the grinding mixture with the eyedropper, remove the collar, dry the work well, and start all over again. If there is only a very small leak, particularly one developed toward the very end of the operation, one just has to keep on adding new abrasive and water as needed.

Grinding jade causes a foam to be generated which may get so voluminous and dense that some of it will have to be spooned out and replaced with freh water and grit.

When the drill has reached its lowest point, it must be raised again. This is done by raising the platform with the wheel attachment and fastening it in the desired position with the setscrew in front of the drill below the drill platform (see Fig. 5-12). It is probably best, even though not absolutely necessary, to shut off the drill while doing this, particularly in the very eartly stages of apprenticeship. The work should be raised in stages of about $^3/8''$ (9.52mm) at a time as the belt will jump off the pulley if it is raised too high in any one step.

When the drill has penetrated about an inch into the work, the core should be removed to do away with some of the friction on the inside of the drill bit. There is an optimum length for the core to be snapped out. If it is too short, it will not break off well. If it is left too long, it will slow down the drilling operation. To accomplish it, the platform

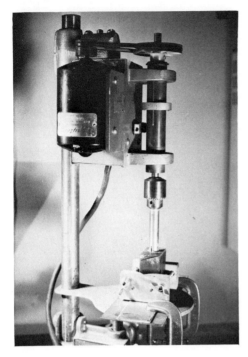

Fig. 5-5 Preform lined up for drilling.

Fig. 5-6 Oversized drawing of hole eases lining up.

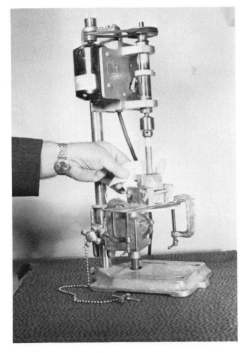

Fig. 5-7 Applying a collar of adhesive.

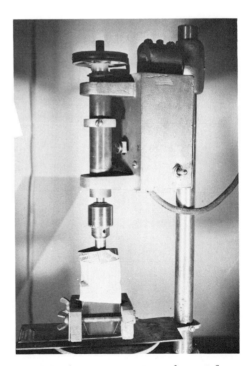

Fig. 5-8 Aluminum strip is used to reinforce collar.

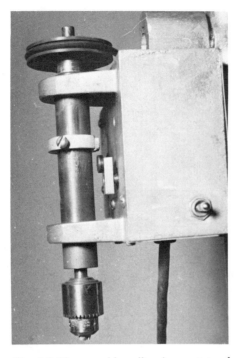

Fig. 5-9 The movable collar does not touch cam.

Fig. 5-10 Moving of cam collar.

Fig. 5-11 Correct adjustment of cam mechanism.

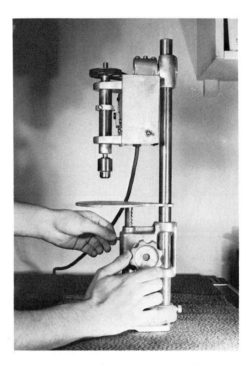

Fig. 5-12 Adjustment of the platform assembly.

should be lowered all the way, the drill pulled up as high as it will go, and the core broken out (see Fig. 5-13). Most of the drilling mud has to be removed for this purpose using a plastic spoon and an eye dropper. Then a small steel wedge is inserted into the groove, given a light blow with a small hammer, and, in most cases, the core will snap off at the very bottom. A square steel nail, sharpened into a wedge point, is a very appropriate tool and easily available (see Fig. 5-14 and Fig. 5-15).

Since the block worked on is $2^1/4''$ (57.15mm) high, the hole to be drilled should be 2'' (50.80mm) deep. This is about all the depth which can be drilled without asking for trouble, using a 3'' (76.20mm) core drill, as it is advisable to keep the drill chuck out of the drilling mud. It is also an optimum depth because the drill table can be raised just $1^1/2''$ (38.10mm) on the Pro-Carva drill. The extra $1/2''$ (12.70mm) is obtained by raising the drill by $3/8''$ (9.52mm) to start with, and then lowering the drill bit in the chuck by the required fraction. If the gemstone blank is much higher and a deeper hole is required, a longer core drill has to be substituted for the 3'' (76.20mm) one.

Someone will ask why a longer core drill was not used in the first place. The answer to this is that the movement of the drill platform determines the depth of the hole which can be drilled unless both the platform and the drilling rig are moved. This, however, may cause a distortion of the hole. Substituting a longer core will permit a greater depth of hole without that danger, but only after the drill has already penetrated fairly deeply.

To replace the core drill, it is released from the chuck and left in the hole. The platform is lowered to its deepest setting. The drill assembly is then swung out of the way by loosening the two screws which hold it to the arm extending from the mast, and the pin between them is removed (see Fig. 5-16). Next, the bit is replaced by a longer one which is inserted into the hole. The drill is swung back and the center pin reinserted, which will secure it in the exact position it was in before (see Fig. 5-17). The longer drill bit is raised from the hole and fastened in the chuck. After tightening the two screws next to the centering pin, drilling may be resumed. It is best if the new drill has seen some use on a previous occasion since the leading edge of a drill bit wears thin in use. If an entirely new bit has to be used, it will be advisable to start grinding in a position a little above the greatest depth achieved by the first drill bit. While it is not applicable in this first project, it goes without saying that on achieving a depth of 2'' (50.80mm) while intending to go deeper by an inch or more, the core would have to be broken off and removed once more.

There are two methods to determine the depth of a drill hole. One of these is to put a bandage about the drill bit at the line to which it is supposed to enter the gem material. This bandage is best made from $1/2''$ (12.70mm) to 1'' (25.40mm) decorator's tape (see Fig. 5-18). Since the lubricant will be murky if diamond core drills are used, or opaque if the drilling is done with silicon carbide, the checking of progress will have to be done by "feel" with a metal point.

The better way is to construct a gauge. To do this, a mast made from a wooden slat about 18'' (457.20mm) long, $1^1/2''$ (38.10mm) wide, and a $1/4''$ (6.35mm) thick, is affixed to a platform consisting of another piece of wood about 8'' (203.20mm) long, 4'' (101.60mm) wide, and 1'' (25.40mm) thick (see Fig. 5-19).

The mast is fastened to the longer side of the platform at exactly right angles and at its very center. The material to be drilled, held either in a vise or dopped to a piece of wood, is then rested on the drill platform, adjusted in such fashion that the top of the gemstone's surface just touches the tip of the drill which, in turn, is set at its lowest point. A line is then drawn on the upright of the gauge stand where the top edge of the drill platform touches it. Next a mark is made above this to denote the depth of the desired penetration (see Fig. 5-19). When the drill platform is raised to this point (see Fig. 5-20),

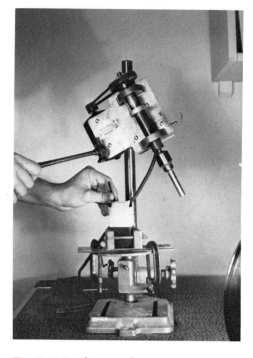

Fig. 5-13 Breaking out the core.

Fig. 5-14 Wedge made from steel nail.

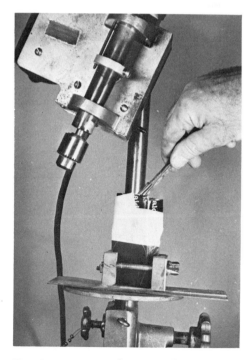

Fig. 5-15 Removing the core with tweezers.

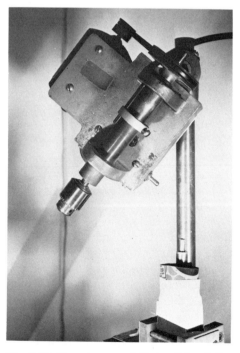

Fig. 5-16 Changing core drills by tilting drill.

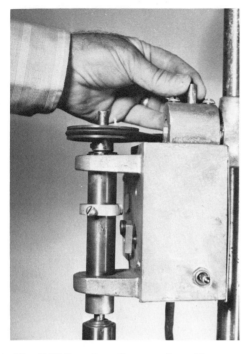

Fig. 5-17 Insertion of center plug will assure correct alignment.

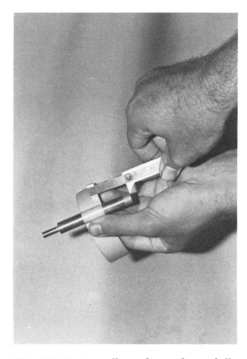

Fig. 5-18 Taping collar to diamond core drill.

Fig. 5-19 Homemade gauge to measure depth of drill hole.

Fig. 5-20 The drill is raised.

and the drill has penetrated into the work so that the drill assembly rests at its lowest point once again (see Fig. 5-21), the hole will be of the desired depth.

Both in the case of the bandage and the gauge, this control will be accurate only if diamond core drills are used which, in suitable material, show no measurable wear from hole to hole. In case metal drills are used in conjunction with silicon carbide, allowance must be made for wearing away of the drill. This varies a little bit depending on the hardness and toughness of the material being drilled, dimensions of the drill bit, and size of grit. This "rate of wear" can be accurately determined by measuring the drill bit before and after use, or it can be estimated from experience if absolute accuracy is not too important. This rate of wear is $1/64''$ (.39mm) for $1''$ (25.40mm) of drilling with a $1/2''$ (12.70mm) drill bit working in jade.

To return to the project in hand, when the depth of $2''$ (50.80mm) or $2^{1}/4''$ (57.15mm) is achieved—as the case may be—the work is removed from the drill by loosening the clamps and the drill bit. The material is taken out of the vise, and the tape collar removed. The remaining core is broken out and the work washed thoroughly (under running water, using a nail brush). The drill bit is then cleaned inside and out.

It will be noted that the bit not only has shortened, but also thinned somewhat. The notches which the manufacturer provided have shortened and may have disappeared altogether. Since they serve to facilitate the introduction of new abrasives, they should be renewed either with a jeweler's saw using a fairly thick blade (see Fig. 5-22), or a cutoff disk in a flexible shaft tool (see Fig. 5-23). In the latter case safety goggles should be worn. To hold the drill bit while it is thus being worked on, it should be held in a chuck. A regular vise would deform the tang of the drill bit. The chuck of a flexible shaft tool, or of a hand drill would be good for the purpose. A dowel of approximately the diameter of the hole is now inserted into it to make sure that it went down as intended (see Fig. 5-

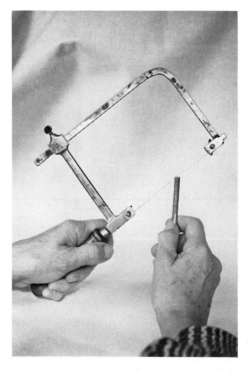

Fig. 5-21 The drill has penetrated and stopped cutting.

Fig. 5-22 Recutting notches with a jeweler's saw.

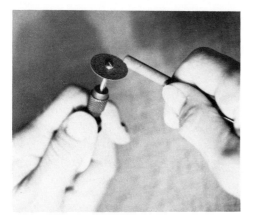

Fig. 5-23 Recutting notches with a cutoff disk in a flexible shaft tool.

Fig. 5-24 Checking depth and direction of hole with a dowel.

24). If the work was not clamped squarely, the whole may be at a slight slant making a re-alignment of the outer shape necessary.

Forming the exterior of the bottle comes next. It is good to remove as much material as possible by sawing as it saves time and material. Sawing may be done by slanting cuts (see Fig. 5-25) or by making a number of parallel incisions and breaking off the resulting fins with a small chisel or screwdriver (see Fig. 5-26).

The presawed blank is then taken to the grinding wheel for shaping. In this we are guided by the outlines previously drawn on the gem blank. While this has been mentioned before, it cannot be said too often that grinding such large blocks is hard on the grinding wheels which will get bumpy in no time, and will have to be dressed frequently. The problem will be alleviated somewhat by using a tool rest to support the material for as much of the grinding as possible. The shaping is nothing else but the fashioning of a large, somewhat complicated, double cabochon. The work around the neck of the bottle is

Fig. 5-25 A snuff bottle blank with saw notches.

Fig. 5-26 The notched pieces have been broken off.

the most delicate part of the operation, entailing the use of the edges of the grinding wheels, one of which should be slightly rounded off for this purpose (see Fig. 5-27). In sanding the neck area, it will help if the sanding cloth is extended a bit beyond the edge of the sanding drum. Polishing should be postponed until the hollowing out of the bottle is completed. It is advisable to plan the curve of the neck so that it will offer a minimum of problems in cutting, sanding, and polishing.

Many people content themselves with doing nothing to the interior of the bottle beyond the initial drilled hole; but more ambitious workers will not rest until the inside of the bottle conforms more or less with the outside profile. The drilling machine may be used for this purpose by tilting it as has been previously described. Hollowing out is done by using abrasive grits with various tools made of anything from mild steel, to copper, to aluminum.

Sperisen (see Bibliography), in his excellent book, recommends ball-shaped tools on fairly long shafts introduced into the drill holes at a slant (see Fig. 5-28). Frances Paul Crafts made two such tools for me, one of aluminum and one of copper. While they were moderately priced, I found that they wear so fast that, even so, the hollowing out operation becomes rather expensive. By scouting around in hardware stores, I found a number of items such as small hinge pins, carriage bolts, and similar things with shanks $1/4''$ (6.35mm) thick or less which could be adapted for this work as they were, or used after a little grinding, filing, and sawing.

There is, of course, great danger that the shank of the tool used in removing the interior will touch and damage the rim on the mouth of the bottle as this work is being done. To obviate this, a protective device has to be made or found (see Fig. 5-29). I made mine by constructing a ring about $5/8''$ (15.85mm) wide of 20 gauge copper, to fit tightly into the opening of the bottle. This, in turn, was soldered to a small square of copper about $1''$ (25.40mm) on edge with a hole in the center as large as the inner opening of the ring (see Fig. 5-30). Such a device can be used over and over. If a grommet of the desired dimensions can be found, it will save the work of manufacturing the neck protector.

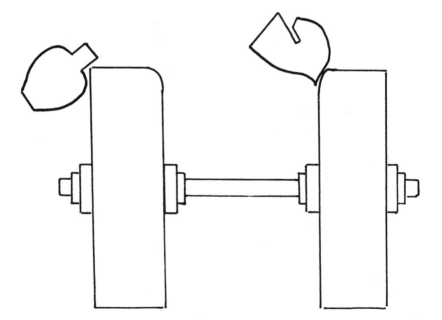

Fig. 5-27 Edges of wheels rounded for carving.

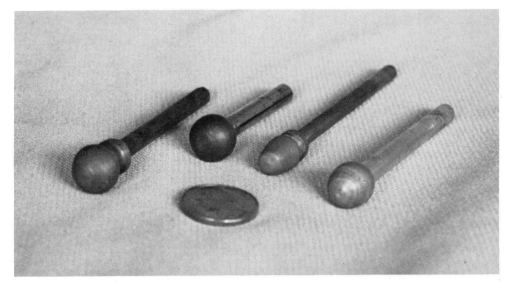

Fig. 5-28 Hollowing out tools (left to right: hinge pin, diamond charged copper tool, worn hinge pin, and aluminum ball tool).

Fig. 5-29 Neck protectors (clockwise from left to right: a homemade device, a grommet, another homemade neck protector, another grommet, a penny for size comparison).

To hollow out the neck area without damage, the gadget is fitted over the opening of the bottle. Sometimes it may be necessary to slip this over the shank of the drill bit before inserting it in the chuck since the working end of the tool may be slightly larger than the hole in the protective device (see Fig. 5-30).

A quarter teaspoon of abrasive is now inserted into the hole of the bottle; water is added to fill it between a half to three quarters way up. The bottle is then held by hand in such a manner that the drill bit is inserted in the hole without touching anywhere. The hand holding the bottle also grasps the neck protector to keep it from coming loose from vibrations during the ensuing operation (see Fig. 5-31). The drill is then switched on. The

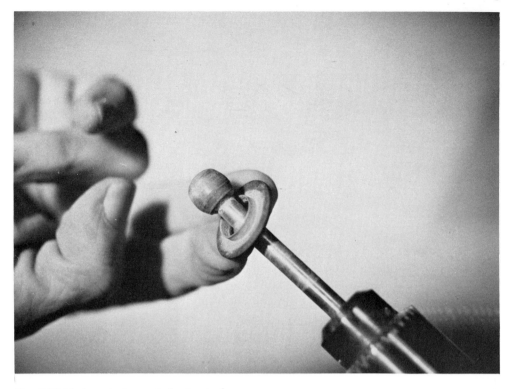

Fig. 5-30 Neck protector on hollowing tool.

cam action is not used in this process and the collar is therefore adjusted as though the machine is to be used as a drill press. The work is moved slowly until contact is made with the grinding part of the drill, about ¹/₂″ (12.70mm) down from the rim, and slowly rotated in one plane to create a shallow groove all around the inside of the bottle at this level. Contact should be fairly firm, but it should be kept in mind that the tool is only the carrier of the abrasive and that too much pressure will be counter-productive. The bottle should be moved up and down at frequent intervals to keep the drill bit wet and the grit mixture stirred up at all times. When a slight indentation has been ground at the level which will constitute the inside shoulder of the bottle, the method of grinding is changed to an up-and-down motion, holding the bottle at a slant in contact with the grinding surface. During this sequence of motion the grinding head should slightly touch bottom at the end of the down movement, which should then be reversed until the previously ground groove in the neck is reached when it should be reversed again. At each such move, the bottle should be turned slightly so as to keep the hollowed out surface as even as possible. In opaque material the extent of the hole can only be determined by feel and visual inspection. In translucent ones, it may be visible, and in transparent ones, it will be visible from the outside. In translucent materials, the thinner the wall left, the better. Jade may be cut to great thinness with impunity, but with other materials it pays to be conservative.

If the interior is to be polished, final grinding should be done with 600 grit or finer. Polishing is only necessary in transparent bottles and is rather tedious. There are, to my knowledge, no commercially made tools available for this work. Sections of wooden dowels may be utilized, fastened with epoxy to a nail 3″ (76.20mm) to 4″ (101.60mm) long (see Fig. 5-32).

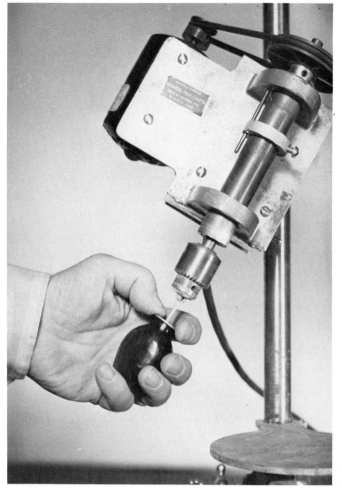

Fig. 5-31 Hand holding bottle and neck protector in place.

Fig. 5-32 Polishing tools made from wood, felt, and leather.

Fig. 5-33 Jade bottle, cut and sanded.

Fig. 5-34 Bottles with various stoppers.

The exact procedure for making one of these is as follows: Two pieces of $1/2''$ (12.70mm) dowel rod are cut $1/2''$ (12.70mm) to $5/8''$ (15.87mm) in length. One of these is drilled with a drill of the diameter of the nail being used. The top of the hole is widened with a larger drill bit or a countersink bit so that the nail head can be accommodated in the opening. The nail is inserted, glued into place with epoxy, and the undrilled piece of wood epoxied to the top of this assembly. Variations of this tool may be made by using small pieces of sole leather or a small felt plug (made for use with flexible shaft tools) instead of, or in addition to, the top part of the wood.

It is easy to polish the inside of the neck only. For jade bottles, 1200 diamond grit on one of the tools described, or simply on a small section of $1/4''$ (6.35mm) diameter dowel stick, will serve. On other materials, sanding may be done by using one of the wooden tools with 600 or 1200 silicon carbon grits, and polishing with one of the small felt buffs mentioned using standard polishing materials. In polishing the outside of bottles made from gemstones other than jade, felt wheels, either run horizontally or vertically, are a great boon as they yield easily to the contours of the work (see Fig. 5-33).

Stoppers for the bottles are best made from silver with a cabochon of the same material or matching gemstone fastened to it with epoxy or set into a bezel. The stoppers may also be ground entirely of gem material. To do this, a block large enough is dopped to

80

wood or plexiglass. This block should be roughly preformed into a cylinder or square slightly wider than the outside diameter of the bottle's neck, or quite a bit wider if a flaring top is intended. It should have one flat surface into which the drill is to enter. It is then suitably centered and clamped into place. A collar is provided, and a hole drilled $1/2''$ (12.70mm) deep. The drill should have an inside diameter $1/16''$ (1.58mm) larger than the inside diameter of the bottle neck. For example, a drill bit with an outside diameter of $1/2''$ (12.70mm) will leave a hole $9/16''$ (14.28mm) wide. Conversely, a drill with an inside diameter of $5/8''$ (15.87mm) will leave a core $9/16''$ (14.28mm) in width. This core is then freed by making a saw incision all around until it reaches the hole. The bottle top is then finished by the usual cabochon methods. In the final fitting of the stopper it must be borne in mind that holes drilled by core drills are wider at the level where the drill enters than at the bottom of the incision. Therefore, the end of the stopper must be thinned ever so carefully. Grinding on the wheel will accomplish this, but a much more foolproof way is to coat the stopper and the inside of the bottle neck with abrasive mixture, using oil, water, or Carbopol as carrier for the grit. The stopper is then turned by hand until a perfect fit is obtained. To test this, fill the bottle with water and turn it upside down. It should not leak. Our bottle is now ready for snuff, perfume, or display.

6
Making Gemstone Spheres

Making a sphere does not call for any display of artistic talent, but it is a splendid exercise in the use of the saw. It is also a good test of the prospective carver's patience and willingness to stick with an exacting and somewhat tedious job. It needs, moreover, only a very moderate investment, to wit: some short pieces of cast iron pipe and pipe caps (see Fig. 6-1). These items can be purchased at any hardware store, from plumbers, or plumbers' supply shops. The pipes come ready cut and threaded on two ends in short lengths called nipples. The shortest length which can be purchased in anything above 1¹/₂″ (38.10mm) in diameter is 3″ (76.20mm). It can be used as it is, or cut in two, if a friendly plumber can be found. He has a special tool to do just this job. It could theoretically be done with a hacksaw, but the result would most likely not be accurate. The caps have to be pierced in their exact center to fit on a horizontal spindle such as that of a flat lap, tub-type machine or faceting setup. The hole can either be smooth or threaded. In the first instance, it will have to be held between two nuts, in the latter, it has to fit the threading on whatever machine is going to be used. Any machine shop or a kind and knowledgeable friend with a lathe can do this work. The inner diameter of the pipe used should be a little smaller than the desired sphere. For example, a 1¹/₄″ (31.75mm) to 1¹/₂″ (38.10mm) inner diameter pipe will be suitable for a 1³/₄″ (44.45mm) sphere, or a 2″ (50.80mm) inner diameter pipe for a 2¹/₂″ (63.50mm) sphere.

A solid piece of well-patterned gem material such as snowflake obsidian or rhodonite of suitable dimensions is then sawed into a cube. In laying out the design for this, an indelible ink felt tip pen, a thin, preferably stainless steel ruler, and a carpenter's trysquare will come in handy.

Unless there is already a large enough flat surface, a saw cut will have to be made to establish one. On this existing or newly sawn surface are then drawn two lines parallel to each other, the insides of which are separated by the distance desired for the diameter of the planned sphere. The blank is then mounted in the saw vise so that the lined flat surface is at right angles to the jaws of the vise, and the two marked lines parallel to the saw

Fig. 6-1 Pipe nipples and caps for making spheres.

blade (see Fig. 6-2). For the first lineup, the trysquare is used, for the second, the steel ruler (see Fig. 6-3) or a piece of wood about 1″ x 1″ (25.40mm) and 8″ (203.20mm) long.

It will be a great advantage if the chunk of rough is large enough so that the saw cuts along the two lines mentioned can be made without reclamping the material. The first cut is then lined up so that the steel ruler, held along the side of the blade next to the vise,

Fig. 6-2 Trysquare lines up preform at right angle to saw blade.

Fig. 6-3 Strip of wood lines up preform parallel to saw blade.

covers the first black line (see Fig. 6-4). For the second cut, it is held on the side away from the vise covering the second line. The result will be a block just a tiny mite wider than needed. The sawing is then repeated at right angles to the first two cuts in the same manner. The last saw cut is then made opposite to the first one after careful measurements, lining up the cube once more by use of the trysquare (see Fig. 6-5). Once the cube has thus been sawn it is rechecked with a gauge or, if that is lacking, with a C-clamp set to the required measurements. If deviations are found, they are corrected by grinding.

Then an octagon is constructed on paper, and all sides of the cube marked into oc-

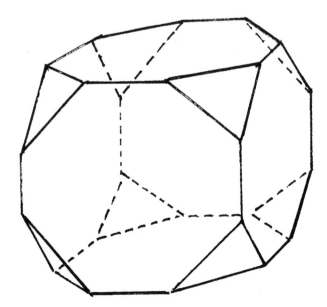

Fig. 6-4 Blank for sphere with corners cut away, leaving six octagonal and eight triangular surfaces.

tagons with the help of the pattern (see Fig. 6-6). Opposite corners of these octagons on all planes of the cube are then connected by lines, forming four cross patterns, the centers of which will be squares. Then the corners of the cube are sawn off, first one way, then at right angles to the previous cuts so that a roundish, many-cornered preform results. (This will be bounded by three chains of eight equal sized squares crossing each other at right angles—see Fig. 6-7). Opposite squares should be equidistant from, and exactly parallel to, each other. Again, the gauge or C-clamp is used to check this, and corrections made, if necessary, on the grinding wheel.

Now the whole shape is painted with white paint to make subsequent marking more visible. White marking ink may be substituted for the paint and is, in fact, preferable because it dries immediately. It is used by machinists in laying out projects on metal, and is available from larger hardware stores, particularly if they supply machine shops. If not

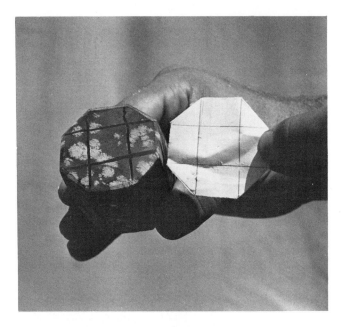

Fig. 6-5 Paper template and preform after four saw cuts.

Fig. 6-6 Three strips, each with eight squares.

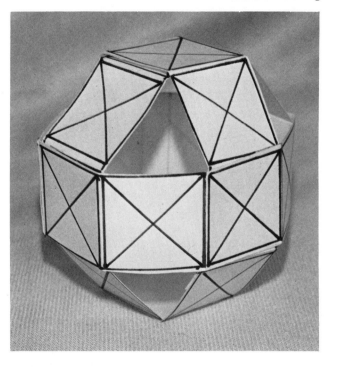

Fig. 6-7 The three strips inter-
secting each other at right angles. This is what the preform of
the sphere will look like before
final rounding off.

available locally, it can be purchased from Arrow Profile Company, 321 W. 10 Mile Rd.,
Hazel Park, MI 48030.

The chains of squares are then outlined with the marking pen, then their centers established by connecting opposite corners.

The centers of the St. Andrew's crosses thus established will be the last points removed in the ensuing grinding. It will be advisable to do this systematically, first grinding
in one direction, then at right angles. Frequent checking with the gauge will be necessary.

When as close an approximation to a globe as possible has been achieved, the pipe assembly is brought into play. For this purpose it is mounted on the spindle. Many spindles
of faceting and tub machines are not threaded all the way. A short piece of tubing, or a
wooden or plastic lap must, in that case, be inserted under the grinding assembly. Then
the pipe is stuffed nearly to its top with closely wadded newspaper or rags. The very uppermost end is filled with a mixture of silicon carbide grit and water, or better yet, with a
mixture of silicon carbide and Carbopol jelly. The preformed sphere is then held on top of
this revolving setup, either just by hand (see Fig. 6-8), or, if larger than 2½" (63.50mm),
with the help of another piece of pipe.

The machine should be run at motor speed (1750 rpm) if speed changes are available.
The preform has to be moved in all directions so as to permit the grit-charged edge of the
pipe to grind away all the high spots. If the preform is well shaped, there will be no visible gaps between it and the top of the pipe. If such spots are showing, however, the
preform should be allowed to stay on the revolving machine for fifteen to twenty minutes.
Then it is washed and inspected.

There will be many areas which are smoother than the rest and some which have not
been touched by the edge of the pipe. If such rough spots are prevalent, it will pay to go
back to the wheel to grind away the smooth spots. If this has been done correctly, a second application of the pipe plus grinding mixture will hopefully show that the real high
spots have been eliminated and there will be no more gaps visible between the preform

1111111111111111

Fig. 6-8 Pipe assembly and preform in place for grinding.

and pipe edge. This does not mean necessarily that the perfect sphere has been achieved. Close examination will probably show that low spots still exist and are visible even without removing the cutting mud. They will appear as rough spots while the rest of the sphere is covered by smooth surfaces showing faint parallel lines made by the edge of the pipe in the thin layer of drilling mixture. Grinding must continue until all the rough places are eliminated.

Toward the end this operation will go faster than in the beginning because the pipe will conform to the spherical shape of the material. This will also mean a very sharp edge forming at its top. Hands must be kept away from this or nasty cuts may result. Many sphere cutters take away this sharp edge from time to time by means of a file. The grit used is worn down fairly fast and must be added continuously in small amounts. Water, of course, also has to be added as it evaporates. This is best done by means of an eye dropper. If the sphere is fairly small—from 1¹/₂″ (38.10mm) to 2″ (50.80mm)—300 grit is used for a start; for larger spheres, 100 grit may be needed in the beginning. For a pre-polish, 600 grit is usually fine enough. The pipe must be emptied and washed for each change in the size of the abrasive.

The spheres may be sanded on a conventional sander and polished on the regular leather or felt buffs used for cabochons. Dopping the globe for this last operation is recommended, but not necessary. It is also possible to polish on the pipe assembly by stretching a piece of soft leather over the top of the pipe. In this case, the sharp edge of the pipe must be filed off as, otherwise, the leather will not last very long. I always line the pan of the grinding machine with old rags so that should I lose control of the sphere, it will not be ruined by touching the hard metal of the tub.

According to J. H. Howard, in his *Revised Lapidary Handbook*, a horizontal spindle can be used for sphere cutting, but to my mind it has a number of disadvantages such as rapid loss of water and grit and lesser control of the material, particularly where large spheres are concerned. There are also special sphere cutting machines built which are expensive and too specialized to fit into the frame of this book.

7
Making Gemstone Beads

Beads are small pieces of material pierced in order to be strung. The manufacture of beads is probably one of the oldest lapidary accomplishments of mankind. Beads may be made of all kinds of material and in all kinds of shapes, from random to round, and from very simple to the most elaborate. The greatest number of beads made and worn, however, are round.

Commercial round gemstone beads are the product of some version of a beadmill. A beadmill is a tub with one stationary, and one rotating surface in which preformed pieces of gemstone, by use of abrasive, are ground to perfect roundness and smoothness. They may also be polished in the same machine with different lap insets and charges of polishing agent. For the amateur the beadmill has only limited attraction as it will make only one size of bead in one charge. The operation is actually an industrial process similar to tumbling. The beadmill is also a relatively expensive piece of equipment which can be used for only a single purpose.

A much more challenging way to make beads is to carve each one by hand. This is a fairly laborious and exacting undertaking if the idea is to make enough beads for a necklace of even moderate length. The beads produced by this method will very likely not stand up to being measured on a micrometer. As long as they are fairly globular and good to look at, slight irregularity is, in my opinion, more of a plus than a minus as it testifies to the fact that they are handcarved rather than products of a purely mechanical process.

The first step in the manufacture is the sawing of blanks. A great effort should be made to get these preforms as nearly cubical as possible (see Fig. 7-1). Making the beads fairly large will reduce the number of holes to be drilled, but, of course, will also call for more work in rounding, sanding, and polishing each bead so that the time consumed will probably be the same for a necklace of a given length in either size bead. Unless the carver has extraordinary skill, it will be advisable to plan on a necklace of graduated beads, as it will be impossible to get all the beads to come out the same size unless one is willing to manufacture a great number of spares. One should prepare a few extra cubes,

Fig. 7-1 Blanks for beads.

however, in any case. Provision should also be made to have enough material for more preforms should one have bad luck during the process of manufacture, since the sawing will, in all likelihood, produce only very few really perfect cubes. In the long run, it will pay off to spend all the effort necessary to see that the bead blanks are ground to true squareness.

The important measurements are the distances from the center of each side of the cube to the center of the side completely opposite on the cube. Once the preforms are as exact as they can be, they are marked by lines drawn from corner to corner of each square (see Fig. 7-2).

The resulting markings of the six center points are the last thing to be ground away in the making of a round preform. If the beads are $1/2''$ (12.70mm) or larger, they will be held by hand for this work. I have found it easiest to start with grinding away the corners of the cube as evenly as possible, resulting in a polyhedron with six octagonal and eight triangular surfaces (on the cutaway corners).

Fig. 7-2 A bead blank lined for preforming.

The polyhedron is then ground into a cylindrical shape, doing away with four octagonal surfaces during this operation. The blank is then turned at right angles and ground round in this direction, removing the remaining two octagons. We have now a rather overstuffed cushion with four edges. Turning the blank 45 degrees, one of these edges is then trimmed away. The other one is next to go, leaving us with a fair approximation of a sphere (see Fig. 7-3). It is important to keep the blank as symmetrical as possible, but even so, there will be many protuberances to be trimmed off. Frequent inspections will help in getting these ground down. It will be found that touch is as great a help in discovering unevenness as sight. A template with many sizes of round holes will also aid in this work. After about the tenth bead, most people will be able to omit the time-consuming markings of each bead and still come up with fairly good globes.

In the beginning, the preform is held with two or even three fingers of each hand. Toward the end, when the bead is nearly round, it is best held with two fingers of the dominant hand, assisted by just the index finger of the other. At this stage, it is held very lightly and rotated rapidly. A well dressed wheel will help in avoiding the possibility of having the bead torn from the carver's hold. Should this happen, however, the machine should be stopped before attempting to retrieve it to avoid injury.

There is also another way of turning out globular beads, which is a little more mechanized and much slower. After an approximation of the sphere has been reached as described earlier, the gemstone ball is dopped on a nail with enough wax to hold it securely, but in such a manner that approximately two-thirds of the preform is exposed. A $^1/_2''$ (12.70mm) diameter, 3" (76.20mm) long piece of galvanized pipe called a half inch nipple, which you can buy in hardware stores, is then stuffed with rags, leaving just about $^1/_2''$ (12.70mm) at its top empty. This hollow space is then filled with a mixture as thick as heavy cream of 100 grit and Carbopol or water. The former is better as it dries out more slowly and is less apt to be thrown off in the grinding operation. The nail with the preform is then inserted in the handpiece of a flexible shaft tool or in the gem drill tilted for carving (see Fig. 7-4). A speed regulator should be used in either case. The flexible shaft setup is preferable as it will allow movement of both the bead and the pipe with the grinding compound. If the gem drill has to be used, the movable collar should be fastened at the very top to inhibit any up or down movement of the drill.

The bead is then pushed into the pipe nipple loaded with grinding compound and started, slowly at first and then speeded up as grinding progresses. The relation of bead

Fig. 7-3 Progress of blank in five stages (from left to right: a cube; cube with corners ground away; rounded in one direction; rounded at right angles to this; the bead roughly shaped.

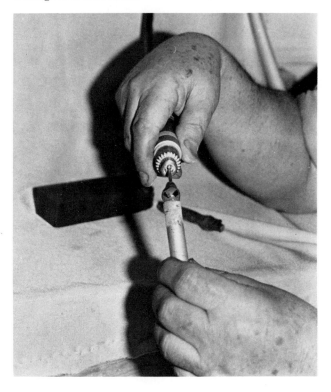

Fig. 7-4 Flexible shaft and pipe
setup for forming beads.

and pipe should be changed continuously at a fast pace. Frequent inspection is impera-
tive. If the surface of the preform shows that most of it is being smoothed, with only a few
small spots which are not affected because they are a little lower than their surroundings,
all is well, and the grinding is repeated until they, too, are eliminated. If large parts of the
surface being worked are left rough, it will be necessary to go back to the grinding
wheels.

The surfaces, which are smooth, are then ground away to bring all the bead's surfaces to a uniform level. The preform is then reinserted in the flexible shaft or drill chuck,
and smoothing is attempted once more. If still out of shape, the corrective grinding will
have to be repeated. Once more than half of the preform is smooth, it may be sanded and
polished on conventional machinery. After this, it is turned over 180 degrees and the bottom part undergoes the same treatment. With luck, we now have a fairly exact bead (see
Fig. 7-5). It would probably not stand up to micrometric measurements, but if it is
visually acceptable, drilling is the next step.

The best way to do this is with the help of a "bead gripper" manufactured by Crown
Manufacturing Co. (see List of Suppliers). This is a little tub-like container with a removable inset in which a bead can be held until it is partly drilled through, then turned over
to be drilled from the opposite side so that the holes meet (see Fig. 7-6). This will avoid
the splintering which would invariably occur if the drill were permitted to pass through
the bead in one operation. The description which comes with the instrument when you
buy it claims that beads up to 5/8" (15.87mm) may be processed, but to do so I had to
replace the 3/4" (19.05mm) screws furnished with the device with 1" (25.40mm) screws.
The 3/4" (19.05mm) screws only held preforms up to 9/16" (14.28mm) in diameter. The
jaws of the little vise should always be parallel and well tightened when holding the beads
for drilling. Even so, I found that the device is not absolutely precise (at least the one I

Fig. 7-5 Beads mounted on nail for shaping.

own is not). Occasionally the inset will jam somewhat and has to be wriggled loose, and the two holes may diverge by a few degrees. This may be due to the fact that the preform is not one hundred percent exact. But, even so, they always do meet, and of all the possible methods to do this work, I have found this the most practical.

The drilling can be done with diamond drills or with metal drills and silicon carbide. For the necklace described here, I used a sintered-type diamond drill (2mm) which had seen previous service, and cost in the vicinity of $4. After going through about forty jade beads, about ⅝" (15.87mm) in diameter, it shows little wear and is in good shape for further use. Only water was used as a lubricant, filling the tub of the bead gripper so that the insert holding the head was barely submerged.

If metal core drills are employed, the beads should be clamped with a little putty between bead and clamp on both sides (see Fig. 7-7). A very small amount of grit is then in-

Fig. 7-6 Bead gripper with bead in place.   Fig. 7-7 Steel sash putty inserted around bead.

serted in the hollow recess on top of the insert which holds the preform. Water is added and the drill is ready to work. The putty will insure a watertight bond between bead and holding device.

Either solid or small core drills may be used. Brads $1^{1}/_{2}''$ (38.10mm), with their heads ground or cut off, may be used for solid drills. For core drills, steel tubes of very small diameter are obtainable (from Frances Paul Enterprises—see List of Suppliers). These are 12" (304.80mm) long and may be inserted full length into the inside of the drilling quill with just as much of their length protruding on the working end as is needed. These, however, may give a little trouble if the core breaks off while the drilling goes on. One then has the choice of using them as solid core drills, trying to push out the core with a piece of wire, or cutting off the jammed end.

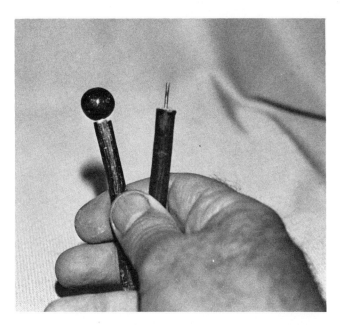

Fig. 7-8 Bead holders made from dowels and brads.

Fig. 7-9 Line up of formed beads.

Only for the metal bits used with silicon carbide is the cam mechanism in action. While not absolutely necessary, it is a help to use the "depth gauge" to determine the penetration of the drills into the bead preform. Since the drill, once set, will work automatically, the operator can shape additional beads while the holes are being made.

After all the little spheres are shaped and drilled, they are sanded and polished on standard equipment. For this purpose they may be held on "pin holders" made by pushing or hammering the ubiquitous 1½" (38.10mm) brads partly into 3" (76.20mm) pieces of hardwood dowels and then pinching or grinding their heads off (see Fig. 7-8). The protruding pieces of nail must be shorter than the diameter of the beads being worked on. Quite a few of the beads may have to be corrected a little before they are sanded as inspection reveals irregularities after they are impaled on the pin holders. The beads should be able to revolve freely on their axis, but for most of the grinding, sanding, and polishing, it is best to control their spinning by braking them with the fingers of one hand so that they will rotate only very slowly. If allowed uncontrolled movement, they might be either heated too much, or thrown off the holder and thus be damaged or lost. Toward the very end of each operation they may, however, be permitted to spin more freely as long as they do not get out of control. The string of beads in Figure 7-9 is a little over 18" (457.20mm) long and consists of thirty beads.

8
Making a Bracelet and Rings from Hard Gemstone

Bracelet

To make a jade bracelet, a blank about ¹/₂″ (12.70mm) thick, and at least 3″ (76.20mm) by 3″ (76.20mm) is needed. It is best to saw or grind the blank to an exact square. Then apply to its center a piece of marking or adhesive tape. This will give a grip to the compass point needed to draw the circles required in the following construction. Mark the exact center point of the blank on this tape, and around it draw two circles, one 2¹/₂″ (63.50mm), and one 3″ (76.20mm) in diameter. If a core drill of 2¹/₂″ (63.50mm) outer diameter and a large drill press to use it in are available, employ these to remove the inside core. If not, use a smaller core drill, but if possible, one not less than 2″ (50.80mm) in diameter. This is the largest core drill that a small drill press, such as the Pro-Carva Gem Drill, will swing.

Mount the blank on a piece of wood with dopping wax. The wood should be larger than the blank, but small enough to be held on the drill table. The wax should support the gemstone in the places which will be pierced by the drill, but should not protrude beyond the edges of the blank. A collar of tape is then fastened around the blank to retain the drilling mud or water coolant. To be doubly sure, a circle of steel sash putty is applied around the base of the blank covering the lower edge of the tape and bonded to the supporting wood.

The object is now lined up on the drill platform so that the core drill is centered in the inner circle. A teaspoon of 100 or 200 silicon carbide grit and a small amount of water are added, and the core drilled out. The assembly is then removed from the drill table and the core which will stick to the dopping wax support is removed by using a small wedge. This core may be used in making pendants (see Chapter 15) or for any other purpose the carver pleases.

There remains quite a bit of stone to be removed within the 2¹/₂″ (63.50mm) circle. This can be ground out or partly removed by further drilling. I prefer the latter method because I believe that it saves time. A mixture of plaster of Paris (two parts plaster to one part of water) is prepared and the cavity from which the 2″ (50.80mm) core was removed is filled to the level of the gemstone. Then, at least two more cuts are taken removing two or more thin crescent shapes of jade from within the 2¹/₂″ (63.50mm) inner ring. After this, the blank is removed from the supporting wood and any excess of jade remaining within the 2¹/₂″ (63.50mm) circle is ground away using the homemade grindstones on the drill or carver. The jade blank is held by hand for this operation, water being supplied by a sponge.

When the inside has been ground out evenly, the outside is shaped on a large grinding wheel into a perfectly round hoop. Much of this work can be done by resting the gemstone on a tool rest, thus dressing the grinding wheel for the ensuing rounding off. This also is done on the large wheels. Some sources recommend to fit the bracelet with an inside core of wood to strengthen it for the grinding, sanding, and polishing, which is to come. I have not found this necessary, but if there should be any suspicions of possible weakness in the material, it might be a worthwhile precaution.

The sanding and polishing of the outside of the bracelet is done on the largest setups available. The inside is best sanded by use of Cratex cylinders. The finish which they leave may be all that is desired, but if a higher polish is desired, muslin buffs with one micron alumina may be used. These buffs can be either the small kinds swung on the drill or flexible shaft, or larger 2″ (50.80mm) buffs used on a tapered spindle as in silver polishing.

Rings

Rings are done in a manner very similar to the making of the bracelet, except that their small diameter renders the work a little easier. It is best to start with a square or oblong blank, dependent on the design, of even thickness. The blank is marked for drilling and fastened to a small piece of wood or plastic. If the ring is for a particular person, it is best to ascertain the size desired and use the appropriate core drill. Ring size 6, for example, requires one of ⁵/₈″ (15.87mm) outer diameter. It may be necessary if the exact size drill is not available to enlarge the hole by a bit of grinding either with Mizzy wheels or with homemade grinding wheels. Once the inside of the ring is of appropriate size the outside is shaped. The ring may be just a simple circle of stone but there are many other and more interesting versions possible. The most useful material for rings is, again, jade, as it will resist hard knocks more efficiently than any other material, but many other gemstones may be used by themselves, or if the skill is available, in conjunction with silver or gold linings and ornamentation.

9
Carving a Duck

Carving a duck is a bit more difficult technically than any work so far undertaken. It is the first carving in the round and requires extensive saw shaping as well as some use of the small rotary tools. A blank, 4" (101.60mm) by 2" (50.80mm) by 2" (50.80mm), is required. For Figure 9-1, a good grade of unakite was used. I had previously carved this figure in wood and used the small wood sculpture as a model. As recommended in the general instructions, a modeling clay figurine should be made to acquaint the carver with the general configuration of the bird (see Fig. 9-2). This will also serve to figure the proper balance of the little statue which could easily topple over if this has not been calculated properly. From the clay figure, a paper pattern is made both of the side view and the top view which is transferred to the stone block. An aluminum line will do, but an outline of waterproof ink is preferable.

The block can then be preformed with either a trimsaw or an overhead saw. Then the preform is taken to the grinding wheels. As in all such carving, the largest tools possible should always be used. We begin on the 8" (203.20mm) grinding stones using the edge of the wheel where indicated (see Fig. 9.3). While one can start anyplace, it will be easiest to start with shaping the duck's back. The breast may require the use of a 6" (152.40mm) by ¹/₂" (12.70mm) wheel which can be mounted either horizontally in one of the tub machines, or vertically on a homemade carving setup. If these instruments are not available, we must resort to the small homemade grinding stones held, preferably, in the gem drill chuck or, if small enough, in a flexible shaft tool. In the latter case, some provision should be made to hold the handpiece stationary to avoid excessive deformation of the grinding disk. If the 6" (152.40mm) wheel is used in the tub machine, a few washers with ¹/₂" (12.70mm) holes inserted under the grinding stone will allow for more clearance from the bottom of the tub to the lower edge of the wheel. If the drill or flexible shaft tool is used, water can be brought to the work with a sponge, and the carving performed over a shallow bowl of water in which the work and the tool are immersed at frequent intervals. The tool should not be in motion when this is done to spare the carver

97

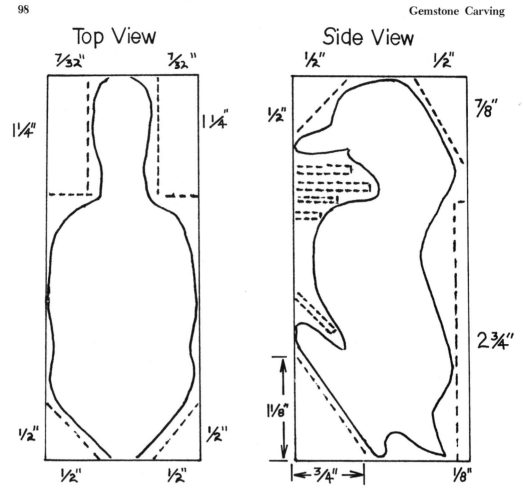

Fig. 9-1 Diagram of duck figure, side and top views.

Fig. 9-2 From left to right: wooden model, clay model, and finished duck.

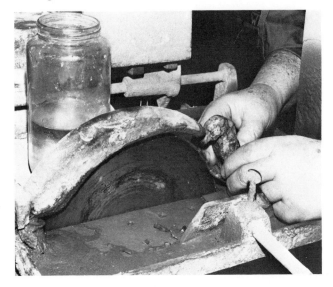

Fig. 9-3 A trimsaw is used for carving.

Fig. 9-4 The finished duck.

a good wetting. It will also keep the electrical machinery from being damaged by spray. The region of the lower beak and the neckline as well as the sharp angle between stomach and the feet of the duck will have to be cut with the Mizzy wheels swung either in the drill chuck or a flexible shaft tool. If diamond bits are used, it is a must to have plenty of water at the cutting spot since a diamond point running dry for more than a second or two may be damaged or even ruined. Here the drip bottle method is the most reliable water supply.

Most sanding of this figure can be done on the large wheels. The small 1/4" (6.35mm) and 1/2" (12.70mm) sanding drums may be used where the larger ones will not reach. Sanding disks, 3/4" (19.05mm), and Cratex wheels and cylinders also are very helpful at times. In the neck area, a piece of tightly rolled sandpaper, either crimped on itself, or rolled over a small dowel or nail and wielded by hand, will do yeoman service. For polishing, felt disks, both large and small, cannot be excelled.

Incidentally, there is no better way to carve the eyes than with a very small (1/8"— 3.17mm) diamond core tool. After marking the spot for the eye with a marking pen, a very short application of this drill will make a perfectly circular impression, which would be hard to achieve by any other means. This is concededly a very expensive tool, but it will earn its keep if the carver intends to do figure carving to even a moderate extent.

10
Carving a Frog

The next project, the carving of a frog, is again a figure in the round. It is a lot more complicated and calls for more, and increasingly intricate detail work. A blank 2″ (50.80mm) by 1¹/₂″ (38.10mm) by 1¹/₄″ (31.75mm) is required (see Fig. 10-1). Plain dark green or snowflake jade are very suitable materials, not only because of their working characteristics, but also because the finished article will really look like a frog.

As usual, the model or paper cutouts of top and side views (see Fig. 10-2) are superimposed on the blank in various ways to find the most economical manner of using the gemstone. By orienting the figure at a slant from one front corner to a diagonally opposite rear corner, for example, it may be possible to get a rough preform by just trimming off two larger wedges. Alternately, an alignment of the frog's main axis, parallel to the long side of the blank, will entail sawing off four smaller, less usable, pieces (see Fig. 10-2a). Next, a horizontal triangular wedge is removed from the front of the blank by two cuts slanted toward each other (see Fig. 10-2b). This may, of course, also be accomplished by parallel cuts (see Fig. 10-2c). This incision will delineate roughly the lower jaw and the front of the forefeet. A similar cut is made in the bottom of the blank to establish roughly the rear line of the forefeet (see Fig. 10-2c). Next, the figure is swathed in adhesive tape to create a reservoir for drilling. The preform is then clamped in a vise, and a ¹/₄″ (6.35mm) hole is drilled at about a forty-five degree slant below the parallel to the lower jaw (see Fig. 10-3). It is aimed to emerge in the area where a wedge has been sawed from the bottom of the blank (see Fig. 10-2c). This hole will eventually be expanded into the space separating the forelegs. The blank now begins to take on the shape of the frog (see Fig. 10-4). A wedge is then sawed, starting on a line about ¹/₂″ (12.70mm) below, and parallel to, the top line at the rear of the blank slanting upward and emerging about 1″ (25.40mm) from the front of the preform. Next, two thin wedges are removed, one from each side of the blank; the cuts beginning about ³/₈″ (9.52mm) in from the rear side corner, slanting outward, and ending about ¹/₂″ (12.70mm) forward of where they began (see Fig. 10-5a). The last in this series of cuts start at the front and just a hair off center of the

Fig. 10-1 Clay model of frog and jade blank.

roughed-out forelegs. These cuts slant outward just a little toward the edges of the drill hole (see Fig. 10-5b).

From here on the shaping is done by grinding. Here, the trimsaw may be used as a grinding wheel when narrow incisions are called for. For example, two such incisions are made where the hindlegs meet the body, others are used to indicate where further grinding is to be done on the sides of the figure. From here on shaping switches over to the largest silicon carbide wheels using the periphery—the edge and the sides of the stone—as the occasion may indicate. When all work of this stage of the operation has been accomplished, the frog is very clearly emerging. Mizzy wheels on mandrels, held in the tilted carver-drill or in a flexible shaft, are next called for. Carving is begun using the largest size (1"—25.40mm). As the wheels wear down, which does not take long, they are used to get into tight places such as the top of the hind feet, the indentations around the hind legs, and contours of the forelegs and forefeet. Fine lines such as the separations of the toes on all four feet and the outlines of the mouth, are incised either with small diamond saws, or cutoff disks. In shaping the head, provision has to be made for the bulges containing the eyes which are so very characteristic. These are now refined, the pupils marked in waterproof ink and then cut exactly as has been done in the duck carving.

Sanding, again, begins on the largest sanding drums utilizing the edges of the cloth whenever possible to get into recesses. Next, the small sanding drums are called for, followed by Cratex point and wheels, and ending up with the small diameter sanding disks which are best used back to back. They lose the charge on their outer perimeter first, but can be trimmed with scissors and are useful to the very end.

Polishing starts again on the largest laps or disks available, working down to small hard leather disks or small muslin buffs held in mandrels.

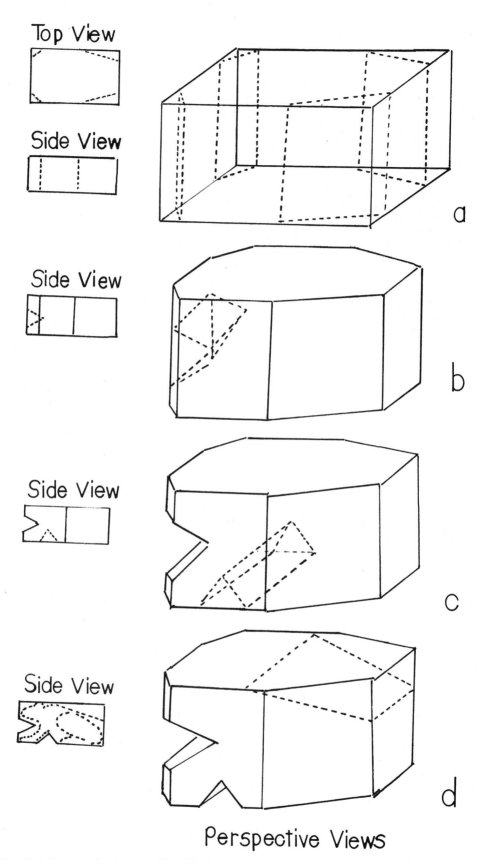

Top View

Side View

a

Side View

b

Side View

c

Side View

d

Perspective Views

Fig. 10-2 Diagram for shaping of frog blank: a) Four corners are sawed off; b) A wedge is sawed from the front; c) Another wedge sawn from bottom of blank; d) A wedge is sawn from top of blank, starting at rear.

102

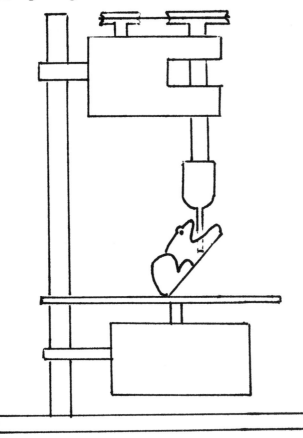

Fig. 10-3 Drilling a hole between front feet.

Fig. 10-4 Frog preform with materials removed.

a   Bottom View

b   Front View

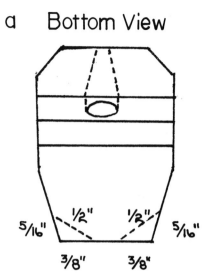

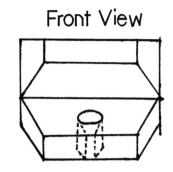

Fig. 10-5 a) Underside, showing cuts at rear and cuts to separate front feet; b) Front view showing cuts separating front legs.

The carver will find that jade presents individual problems practically for each piece or figure worked. Experimenting will be necessary—never forgetting that heat seems to have a beneficial effect both in sanding and polishing. Diamond compounds in various grit sizes will sometimes help when nothing else will. There are a few spots on the frog which cannot be reached by rotary tools. For these spots, hand methods will have to be worked out. A high polish can be justified on this figure as the frog may well be portrayed emerging from a swim.

11
Carving a Bear

Carving a bear calls for the use of all techniques discussed up to now, and can be regarded as a graduation thesis of sorts, promoting the carver from apprentice to journeyman. When it has been done successfully, most further gem sculpture will be just a variation of subject, material, size, and method.

The bear carving calls for a blank 4″ (101.60mm) by 2″ (50.80mm) by 2$^1/_2$″ (63.50mm). The carving described here is made from jade which, according to the seller, comes from Wisconsin and is marketed as Rib River Jade. It is not very outstanding in color but is solid without cracks and works beautifully. It takes a very high polish and is inexpensive. What is more, the seller furnished blocks sawn to given measurements.

The bear is a fairly intricate carving and it pays to get well acquainted with the subject. Some time spent visiting a museum or zoo will be well rewarded. One of the fundamental benefits of carving is that the carver has to learn not only to look at things to recognize them, as we all do, but to look for and retain characteristic details. The best way to accomplish this is to visually study the subject to be reproduced and then make a model from memory. When this figurine has been finished without peeking at the subject, it should be compared with the original and corrected. After doing this a few times, very rapid improvement will be noted.

For the bear I recommend to make at least two full figure models, in addition to a larger scale model of the head. They all will give new insights and each will contain some lines which are more pleasing or significant than the same configurations in others. The best features of all your models should then be united in a final version for which either one of the existing figures might be used or, if preferred, a third version can be turned out. Whichever is chosen, it should be made to the exact scale wanted for the gem carving.

To lend life to the creation about to be called into existence, it will be best to show the bear walking, or possibly with one of his forefeet slightly elevated on a hillock. It should be remembered that bears toe inward, particularly on the front feet. Added motion can be imparted by having the animal turn its head somewhat, which means that a slight angle will have to be given to the shoulders to keep the carving within the limits of the blank. It is fortunate that there are many kinds of bears—brown bears, grizzly bears, Kodiak bears, polar bears, and many others—all of which show somewhat different configurations. Thus, if this first bear is not quite true to any specific type and should unite in its person the characteristics of several species, it will just have to be presumed that it portrays the mésalliance of several ursine tribes.

Now to come to specifics. The blank is converted into a preform by using the saw to remove a wedge in front of the head, a wedge above the back, and a more-or-less rectangular block from the area below the head and in front of the forefeet (see Fig. 11-1). Before proceeding any further, it will be helpful to outline cutting patterns with an indelible ink marking pen on all sides of the blank, and renew them from time to time as they are ground away. Then, material between front and hind legs is removed by either parallel cuts, or a combination of a wedge cut and parallel cuts. Next, the separation between the hind legs is sawed. The lower part of this is a V-shaped incision made by slanting two cuts toward each other at a very narrow angle (see Fig. 11-4). The point of the "V" is then extended by a single saw notch. The front legs need a wider separation which is best made by drilling a hole $3/8''$ (9.52mm) in diameter from a spot below the bear's chest to the opening between front and hind legs (see Fig. 11-3). The top of the hole should be about $1''$ (25.40mm) above the base line of the blank and its end about $1/2''$ (12.70mm) lower. Two parallel, or barely slanting saw cuts, their outer edges $3/8''$ (9.52mm) apart, should then be made toward this hole. They will establish the separation of the front legs. In making these incisions, care must be taken not to saw inadvertently into the underside of the head or into the hind-leg area. Another saw cut may be made to remove a small wedge from the right front end of the preform, assuming that in the finished figure, the bear's head will be turned slightly to the left.

From here on, shaping will have to be done on carving wheels. All of the outside of the figure can be developed on the largest grinding wheels available. Here, the rounded edge of the stone, which has been mentioned repeatedly before, is used extensively to establish the concave curves of the neck and legs. Much of the shaping of the head also can

Fig. 11-1 Diagram of bear with indicated saw cuts.

Fig. 11-2 Clay model of bear and blank presawed.

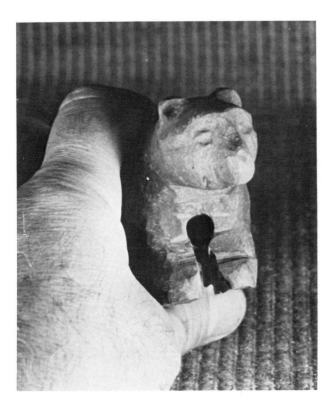

Fig. 11-3 Hole drilled between forelegs.

be done on the big wheels. Generous provisions should be made for the ears, but they should not be refined at this stage, tempting as this may be. Leaving the working out of small details to the last stage of creation is advised in general for all carving work. The reason for this is twofold. In the first place, small protuberances are easily damaged, particularly while large tools are employed and, secondly, it is not uncommon that a figure has to be scaled down or altered during the progress of the work. Then, all the elaborations would have to be done all over.

After all possibilities on the saw and the larger implements have been exhausted, the next small grinding disks are called for (see Fig. 11-4). These are the 6″ (152.40mm) diameter, ¹/₂″ (12.70mm) thick wheels which are usually associated with the tub machines on which they are run horizontally. They may, however, be mounted to run vertically to even better advantage if a carving machine with a ¹/₂″ (12.70mm) horizontal shaft is available.

There are also 6″ (152.40mm) rubber-bonded wheels on the market which can be utilized in the same manner. These are much slower cutting than the ceramic-bonded wheels, but leave a finer surface and are therefore useful for presanding.

The stomach and chest as well as the lower jaw region of the bear can be brought to a nearly final stage on the 6″ (152.40mm) wheels. Naturally these wheels may also be deformed on purpose, just as the larger ones, to achieve special effects. It is easiest to do this with accuracy when they are mounted to run vertically.

The shaping is either done by diamond dressers, or pieces of old silicon carbide wheels are used for this purpose. They are rested on improvised supports such as blocks of wood, or bricks, or whatever else is handy to hold them steady. The 6″ (152.40mm) wheels are followed by 1¹/₂″ (38.10mm) and 2″ (50.80mm) homemade ones which, in their turn, give way to the 1″ (25.40mm) and smaller Mizzy wheels, and silicon carbide points.

When employing these smaller tools in confined spaces, the carver should make sure that they will revolve freely in the area where they are expected to work. If they should

Fig. 11-4 Preform (on left) ready for fine grinding.

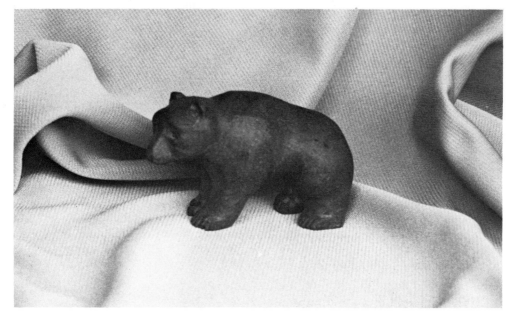

Fig. 11-5 The finished bear.

get jammed, they may tear the material from the carver's grip with the resulting possibility of injury to the operator and damage to the tool and object being carved.

When the figure has assumed satisfactory shape and all blemishes such as remnants of saw cuts and drill marks have been eliminated, the fine detail of the head and claws is worked out. For the latter purpose, cutoff disks, ground down to a diameter of about $\frac{1}{2}''$ (12.70mm), are best. For the elaboration of the face and head, worn down Mizzy wheels are most suitable. For the final refinements such as the modeling of the indentations around the eyes and muzzle and the hollowing out of the ears, diamond tools are recommended. The line of the lower jaw delineating the mouth is best cut with a thin, saw-like diamond disk or a cutoff disk. The ears are first hollowed out and then refined on the outside with a diamond burr $\frac{3}{16}''$ (4.76mm) in diameter and $\frac{3}{32}''$ (2.38mm) thick. The pupils of the eyes are first marked with a dot or small circle of marking ink, and then ground in with a very small ($\frac{1}{8}''$—3.17mm) thin-walled core tool, held in a flexible shaft or carving machine. Instead of the diamond core drill, a small metal tube with loose diamond (200 grit) in oil or Vaseline can be used, but it is much more difficult and time consuming.

After this, the whole figure is sanded to a uniform finish. This is done on conventional sanding belts, Cratex wheels of various sizes and shapes, leather disks, wooden disks, and points charged with assorted grits. Small crevices may be sanded by applying sanding disks (1″—25.40mm—diameter) held back to back in mandrels.

Polishing, in this case, is optional. If desired, leather disks, both soft and hard, and wooden disks and points as well as muslin buffs of assorted sizes from 1″ (25.40mm) to 6″ (152.40mm) may be tried. The standard polishing powders are used. For jade, chromium oxide alone or mixed with Linde A powder works in most cases. When it undercuts, a fine polish occasionally is obtained using diamond compounds on hard leather or hard felt points.

It should be borne in mind that bears in their prime may have a soft sheen to their fur but that no one has ever seen a mirror polish on a live bear. On the one in Figure 11-5, high polish was tried, but removed to go back to a sanded finish.

This is as good a place as any to discuss the desirability of a high polish on gem carvings. Some people seem to think that since gemstone is used it must be shined up until it gleams. To me, this does not make sense. One of the most famous carvings, that of a nude dancer made of chalcedony, in the American Museum of Natural History in New York, is left in a matte texture. This, in my eyes, makes it so much more effective than it would be, had it been shined to a high gloss. However, here, as in all things, there will be a difference of opinion. "Each to his own tastes."

12
Carving a Squirrel

A blank, $2^1/_2''$ (63.50mm) by $2^1/_2''$ (63.50mm) by $1^1/_4''$ (31.75mm), is needed for this carving. It is debatable whether the squirrel image is more difficult to create than that of the bear, and which one should precede the other in the lineup. The squirrel, after much deliberation, was considered to be the more sophisticated and just a bit more difficult to carve.

As in other carvings, after the creation of a model, and the marking of patterns on the blank, a series of saw cuts is made to remove surplus material from around the head. These are indicated in Figure 12-1. Then, saw incisions are made to separate the hind legs from the forepaws, and to separate the tip of the curled tail from the main part of this bushy extremity (see Figs. 12-1 and 12-2). The fins of surplus material are then broken off (see Fig. 12-3) and grinding begins on the large wheel to generate the outlines of the animal figure.

A great effort should be made to give life to the figurine by not pointing all of it in one direction. A squirrel is a very mobile animal.

To convey this, a slight tilt to one side or another should be given to every part of the little body. The head may be pointed in a direction different from that of the forelegs, and the forelegs in a way other than the hind legs. The tail should not only be curled, but should be used to counterbalance the rest of the figure, just as it is employed to balance the live animal.

When the large wheels have done their work, smaller wheels are resorted to. Full size Mizzy wheels are employed to abrade material which the large wheels cannot reach, and as they are worn down, they serve to remove material which they could not touch when full sized. As in all other carving, it may often be possible to return to the larger wheels when protuberances which were in the way, have been removed by the smaller ones. The trimsaw may sometimes be turned to for removing some material which cannot be reached in any other manner. When all these possibilities have been exhausted, cutoff disks are employed to elaborate further detail, such as the separation of the front legs and

Fig. 12-1 Diagram of squirrel with saw cuts indicated.

Fig. 12-2 Model and presawed blank.

the grooves separating the haunches of the hind legs from both body and tail. Small diamond tools are best to delineate the eyes and to carve the interior of the ears. These and worn-down cutoff disks are then employed to separate the fingers and toes of the animal. Squirrel fingers and toes are disproportionately long, a fact that was brought home to me only by a close look at some of the remarkable Audubon prints of these animals.

When all grinding has been finished, sanding may be done by various means with the Cratex wheels performing the main part of the task. Care should be taken not to oblit-

Fig. 12-3 Material between saw cuts has been removed.

erate some of the sharp detail lines which give character to the carving. If necessary, they will have to be retraced after the sanding operation. If the surface gets too smooth, some areas such as the tail may be "roughed up" by appropriately spaced shallow cuts using cutoff disks or thin diamond blades. A moderate polish may be given this figure if desired.

13
Making Ashtrays and Bowls

Many of us when thinking of gemstone ashtrays will conjure up a mental picture of the flat, generally oblong pieces of often very attractive material with shallow indentations which come mostly from Idar-Oberstein, Germany. They are usually about 1/2″ (12.70mm) to 3/4″ (19.05mm) thick, and from 2″ (50.80mm) by 2″ (50.80mm) to 2¹/₂″ (63.50mm) by 3¹/₂″ (88.90mm) on edge. Simple as they look, they are not quite as easy to create without the special equipment which is used to manufacture them in their homeland. However, they are not too difficult, either. Any attractive material of the right thickness and of good pattern and color may be used to make one. "Heels" of fair sized boulders with these qualifications will turn into very attractive ashtrays.

All one has to do is to grind a flat bottom plane parallel to the existing cut. The sawn side is then indented on a grinding stone, after which all the worked areas are sanded and polished. The sides of the object, if they are not marred or disfigured, may be left in their natural state. If no such preshaped rough is available, a slab of approximately the right dimensions may be sawn and ground to the desired shape—a freeform often being preferable to a geometrical pattern.

The indentation of the top is the only area which may offer some little problems. It is best ground in a tub-type machine on a very much-worn down 1/2″ (12.70mm) grinding wheel, the edges of which have been slightly rounded by wear or by shaping with a wheel dresser. It will work best if it has been cut down to a diameter of 4″ (101.60mm) or less. If such a setup is not available, one of the small 1¹/₂″ (38.10mm) or 2″ (50.80mm) homemade grinding wheels run on the gem drill will serve. Sanding can be done on small wood disks charged with a mixture of silicon carbide and water or Carbopol. For polishing, felt wheels or muslin buffs are best.

This, however, is not a real carving project. The sort of ashtray which merits a rating in this category is really a small bowl. It is hard to say where an ashtray leaves off and a bowl begins, so we shall have to leave this decision to the individual.

The procedure is much the same for large and small bowls. It must be said, however

114

reluctantly, that really good sized bowls do call for large drill presses much more powerful than the gem drills available to the average amateur. Bowls made from material 4″ (101.60mm) square and 2½″ (63.50mm) deep will strain his facilities. Smaller dimensions would be much better and will still pose enough of a challenge.

The same material requirements apply to bowls as to other carving projects with the added proviso that the work requires fairly good sized chunks of material which not only should be practically free of flaws, but also of attractive color and pattern. Since the objects created are relatively simple shapes, it is even more important than in figure carving, to make the finished product more acceptable. Nephrite jade, again, is best if a more or less flawless piece of good color can be obtained without mortgaging the family homestead. Jade has the advantage that the walls can be ground very thin without breakage. The resulting translucency will add greatly to the beauty of the carvings. Good second choices are unakite, serpentine, massive epidote, or rhodonite.

There are two different methods for making bowls and ashtrays. However, they do start with the same first steps. For the first version, a blank about 3″ (76.20mm) to 3¼″ (78.55mm) in diameter, and about 1½″ (38.10mm) high is required. It may be possible to purchase a slab of the correct thickness and approximately the right size, otherwise, it will have to be sawn from a larger piece. Many difficulties can be avoided if care is taken to have the top and bottom of this slab exactly parallel. The material is then sawn into a square first and into an octagon next. Then layouts are prepared of the top and bottom of the project on paper (see Fig. 13-1). The top one is a circle of the same diameter as the projected ashtray, 3″ (76.20mm) or 3½″ (88.90mm) with a ⅝″ (15.87mm) hole cut from its exact center. The bottom one is the same circular shape, but the cutout is the size of the intended base which could be about an inch less than the top. The paper disks are fastened to the blank with double stick tape while its sides are still at right angles to the top and bottom planes. Every effort should be made to line them up exactly. If the preform is not exactly round, this will show now; and any material which protrudes beyond the paper templates, as well as the cut-out circles, is painted with either light colored layout ink, or with a waterproof marking pen. The paper cutouts are then removed and the blank is ground to a round shape using the ink marks as guides.

Here, again, we may expect some deformation of the grinding wheels because of the large size of the blank. However, starting with a well dressed wheel and using a tool rest, in addition to moving the work consistently back and forth so as to use the grinding surface uniformly, little trouble will be encountered.

After this, the piece is put into a vise—if one large enough to hold it is available. If there is no such instrument, it must be dopped to a piece of plywood or Plexiglas which has to be large enough to hold the blank, but small enough to be clamped to the drill platform. To make sure of a good bond, the dopping wax should be applied to both the carrier and the stone. Both should be good and hot at the time when they are joined together, or they will come apart some time during the drilling. To hold the heavy preform during heating, a pair of kitchen pliers may be used (see Fig. 13-2). It will also be helpful to use two heat sources such as two alcohol lamps or an alcohol lamp and a one-burner electric stove to bring the two pieces to the desired temperature simultaneously. A collar to contain the lubricant or drilling mud will then have to be constructed as described in the chapter on snuff bottles.

The next step in the operation is hollowing out the inside (see Fig. 13-3). Here is where the difference in procedures begins. Traditionally, this is done by grinding a number of concentric grooves to the required depth with silicon carbide charged, metal core tools. In our case, this would require a series of circular cuts starting with a ½″ (12.70mm) one (the ink mark in the center will help to line this up) and progressing by

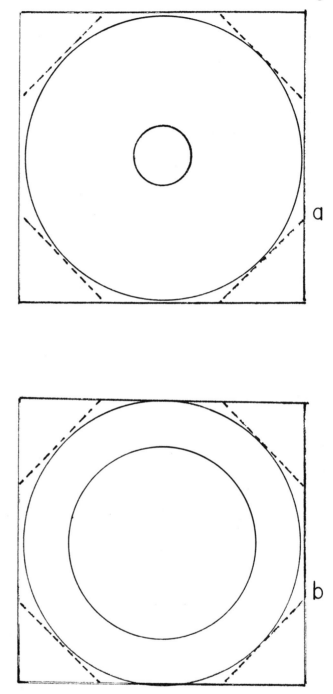

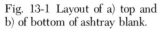
Fig. 13-1 Layout of a) top and
b) of bottom of ashtray blank.

$^1/_4''$ increments to a circle of 2″ (50.80mm). This leaves cylinders a little more than $^1/_8''$ (3.17mm) thick standing between incisions. The depth of these cuts should be about a $^1/_4''$ (6.35mm) less than the thickness of the material. The $^1/_2''$ (12.70mm) center core should be ground $^1/_{16}''$ (1.58mm) deeper than the rest as it will be the starting point from which all the standing cylindrical sections will be undercut. It should be broken out before any of the other circles are begun. Otherwise, when the wedge is inserted between the $^1/_2''$

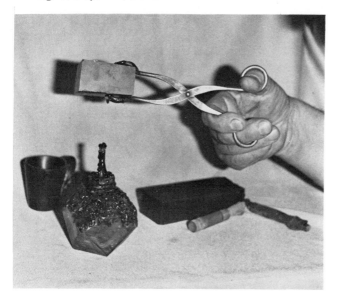

Fig. 13-2 Large block held with kitchen pliers for heating before applying dopping wax to attach the block to the carrier which, while drilling, will hold the blank.

Fig. 13-3 Ashtray blank hollowed out, and two of the ring cores removed.

(12.70mm) center plug and the ⅛″ (3.17mm) wall next to it, it will not remove the thicker core, but instead break the thinner wall.

The broken-out plug is then reinserted in its hole to keep the silicon carbide from settling ineffectively in the empty cavity when making subsequent cuts. For the same reason it is recommended filling the empty space which results from drilling this or any of the other following incisions, with putty as they are finished. It will be easy to clean out the compound when it is not needed any longer.

After all cores are cut, the center plug is removed once again, this time for good. If all has gone well, it has broken out cleanly at its very bottom. If the core is shorter than it is supposed to be, this is a sign that all is not well. Another unfavorable sign would be an uneven break at the lower end of the plug.

In either case, the unwanted material remaining in the cavity has to be milled out. This is best accomplished by use of silicon carbide and a common nail. For this purpose the nail is inserted in the drill chuck upside down. The work is then put back on the drill platform which is raised to a point where the nail's head rests lightly on the bottom of the hole or on the highest point of the material remaining in the cavity.

The so-called "ten-penny" nails which are 5″ (127mm) long, 3/8″ (9.52 mm) in diameter, with a head 1/4″ (6.35mm) wide, are best for the purpose. Most of these nails are straight enough for the purpose, but they must be tested. If the nail retains its shape to the eye of the beholder after the drill is turned on, it is usable, but if it blurs, it must be discarded. To work best, the nail should be modified by filing to roughly true the heads, and by thinning the shaft a little at the head end to establish a right angle where the nail shaft and the head meet (see Fig. 13-4). This work can also be done by holding a piece of discarded grinding wheel against the nail revolving in the drill. A small amount of silicon carbide and enough water to give it a creamy consistency are then dropped in the hole. The platform is then raised to elevate the drill spindle a little. This elevation should be equal to the height of the material in the hole which has to be removed. The blank is moved around to make sure that the bit does not bind any place. Then, the drill is set in motion and the material rotated evenly to keep the bottom of the hole as level as possible. At this stage no pressure is exerted to make the side of the nail head do any cutting. When the drill spindle has reached its lowest point, assuming that the setting was correct, the bottom of the hole should be even over its entire width. When the nail heads thin down during this operation, the nails should be replaced by new ones, but they should not be discarded. They will come in handy for the next operation which is the undercutting of the standing cores.

Undercutting starts as soon as the hole has reached its desired depth all around. Now, the side of the nail head is engaged by using slight lateral pressure as the blank is rotated horizontally, while resting on the drill platform. This will wear away the thin cylinder of jade adjoining the hollow—created by the previous operation—at its lowest point

Fig. 13-4 The second and fourth nail (from left) have been modified for carving.

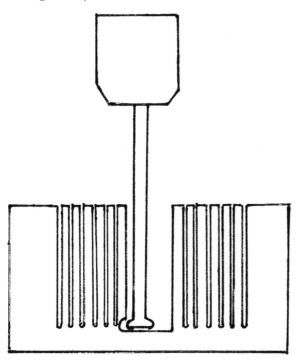

Fig. 13-5 All the core cuts have been made—a nail held in drill upside down is beginning to undercut the standing cores.

(see Fig. 13-5). As this is a tedious operation, one is very much tempted to employ too much pressure, which will only wear the nail head away unnecessarily. Here, the thinned-down nail heads are useful as they will cut a little faster. This is because the thinner cutting edge has to abrade less material.

It is also possible to use tools with heads even thinner than the nails which, of course, work still faster. These tools, unfortunately, are not available commercially, but can be made at home with only a modicum of difficulty. One version of these tools uses copper disks affixed to nails with soft or hard solder. The most satisfactory nail for this purpose is 3″ (76.20mm) long, with a shaft 5/64″ (1.98mm), and a head 5/16″ (7.93mm) in diameter. Before soldering, the nails should be tested in the drill, as mentioned previously, to see that they run true. The copper disks, 1/4″ (6.35mm) to 5/8″ (15.87mm) in diameter, may be sawed from a sixteen or eighteen gauge copper sheet with a jeweler's saw, or may be purchased ready-made at hobby stores. However, the commercially available disks are punched out and, therefore, ever so slightly dished. Before use, they should be hammered flat. To ensure that the disk will be soldered on at right angles to the nail, a jig will have to be made. The drill can be used as a jig as has been explained previously when the manufacture of small grinding wheels was explained.

Another way to make these "undercutters" is by use of nails and steel washers of various sizes (see Fig. 13-6). Choose nails with heads just slightly larger than the inner hole of the washer. Then file them down evenly until their heads can be pressed into the openings so that they will stay there. There is, for example, the 3″ (76.20mm) nail with a shank 5/64″ (1.98mm), and head 5/16″ (7.93mm) in diameter. This nearly fits into a regular 3/4″ (19.05mm) washer, the hole of which is 5/16″ (7.93mm) wide. All these are not micrometer measurements and are subject to some slight fluctuations. In practically every case, the nail heads are "out of round"—wider in one direction than the other—and the holes in the washers taper by a split hair from top side to bottom side. But it is easy in all cases to achieve a fit sufficient for our purpose. As long as the nail will run true and the

Fig. 13-6 Undercutting tools
made from nails and washers.

washer is at right angles to it, the arrangement will work. To achieve this effect, press the
nail head into the hole of the washer and check to see that the two are aligned at a perfect
right angle using the drill press as a jig, then solder or braze the unit together. These
washer-nail undercutters last a lot longer than the copper disks. Because the washer-nail
tools have a lot more clearance than the nails alone, fewer circular grooves will have to be
cut. Instead of progressing by quarter inches from cut to cut, one may advance by half
inches. This will result in thicker cores which have to be undercut.

It is very difficult to tell what progress is being made during this undercutting operation because the drilling mud makes visual inspection impossible. At first, of course, the
tool shank will be some distance from the rim of the hole, but will come closer as the cutting disk bites into the material and is itself abraded in doing so. Probing with a piece of
wire, the end of which is bent into a right angle, will give some information on the depth
of the cut. Experience will tell after a while, how much time approximately, a certain cut
will require. The only way to be sure that the task is finished is to see the ring of gem material on which we are working beginning to move independently. There is one point to
watch out for. If the core being removed is intended for use which will require it to be
polished on its inside, contact of the tool shaft with the gemstone should be avoided.
Using as large a disk on the undercutting tool as will fit the space available is one way of
avoiding such contact.

If one is willing and is financially able to splurge, it is, of course, possible to use small
diamond saw blades on fixed mandrels for this operation. They need only water for coolant, and they work very much faster. I have used such instruments on a number of occasions without their showing measurable wear, but I have never had the nerve to test
how long they can be used before being worn away. I reserve them for occasions when
my patience runs out.

When the first circle has been undercut, the resulting cylinder of gemstone is lifted
out and the operation is repeated on the others in turn until all have been removed, leaving a cavity 1¼″ (31.75mm) deep and 2″ (50.80mm) in diameter.

After this the bottom has to be ground flat, the sides slanted inside and out, and everything sanded and polished. This will be discussed in greater detail a little later in this
chapter.

It is naturally possible to ring in variations on this scheme by using, for example, a $^5/_8''$ (15.87mm) core instead of the $^1/_2''$ (12.70mm) one and skipping the $^3/_4''$ (19.05mm) hole. This will result in a wider gemstone cylinder which can be sawn into ring blanks (about size 6). But it is hard to think of ways to utilize the rest of the material removed. This seems a great waste, since even passable jade is quoted at twenty-five dollars a pound and going up fast.

After some experimenting, I came up with an alternate scheme to do this work. This system calls for the same method in fashioning the blank as before, up to, and including, the fastening of the retaining collar. From here on things are different. Only three circular grooves are needed for hollowing out. Working with a blank approximately 3″ (76.20mm) in diameter, the grooves would measure $^1/_2''$ (12.70mm), $^3/_4''$ (19.05mm), and 2″ (76.20mm) in diameter. The area between the $^3/_4''$ (19.05mm) and 2″ (25.40mm) grooves would be removed by eight holes using $^1/_2''$ (12.70mm) drilling cores. The plugs resulting from this drilling are usable as beads or, when sawn, as cabochons.

Another version of this method would call only for the drilling of two ring cores, one $^5/_8''$ (15.87mm), and one of 2″. The area in between would be removed by drilling six $^5/_8''$ (15.87mm) core holes.

There are a number of other possible combinations the carver may be able to figure out. For a first attempt, the three ring version with the $^1/_2''$ (12.70mm) cores may present the least problems. I shall therefore describe the procedures for it in the following. It should, however, be understood that the holes left by the tools mentioned will not be exactly the same as the bits mentioned, but a little larger. The size of the grooves cut depends on the age of the machine used, the size of the grit employed, and the condition of the drill bit. It also goes without saying that the holes will have to be drilled in stages. (See Chapter 5—Making a Snuff Bottle, for a description of this procedure.) On the other hand, while in snuff bottle drilling we recommend that plugs should be broken out when the holes are about an inch deep, this procedure need not be followed here since most of the holes are only $1^1/_4''$ (31.75mm) deep. The working sequence would be as follows (see Fig. 13-7):

1. Line up the $^1/_2''$ (12.70mm) core drill in the paint-marked center spot. Clamp the work in place.

2. Drill a $^1/_2''$ (12.70mm) hole, $1^5/_{16}''$ (33.33 mm) deep; break out the core but put it back in place.

3. Next, a hole $^3/_4''$ (19.05mm) in diameter is drilled $1^1/_4''$ (31.75mm) deep.

4. Drill a hole $^1/_8''$ (3.17mm) deep with a drill bit 2″ (50.80mm) in diameter. This just serves to line up the holes in the next operation.

5. Drill eight holes $^1/_2''$ (12.70mm) in diameter, $1^1/_4''$ (31.75mm) deep, between the $^3/_4''$ (19.05mm) and the 2″ (50.80mm) circle lining them up as close to each other as possible. The placing of these holes is not difficult if a diamond core drill is employed. There will be a small complication, however, if silicon carbide slurry and diamond drilling are combined. In this case, the collar which has been added previously to retain the abrasive mud is removed, and the piece thoroughly scrubbed. A new collar is applied and partially filled with clear water, just enough to cover the diamond on the core bit. It is then easy to align the work by eye, since after each hole the turbid water is emptied out and clear water is added.

If the grinding is to be done with metal core drills and silicon carbide things become a bit more complicated. It is then necessary to make two templates, one a circle 1″ (25.40mm) in diameter, and one a ring with an inner rim of 2″ (50.80mm) and an outer rim of 3″ (76.20mm) in diameter. They should be made of heavy gauge aluminum foil. It is easier to cut the templates from heavy paper first, and then use these as guides for cut-

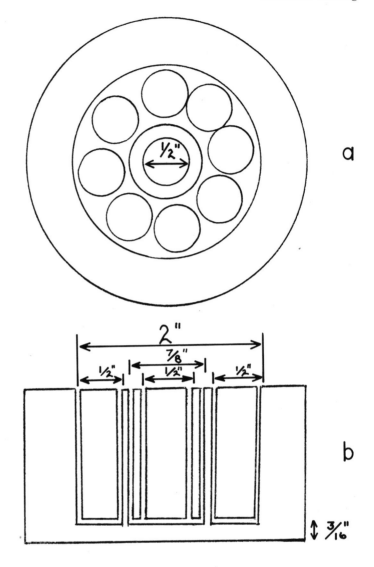

a

b

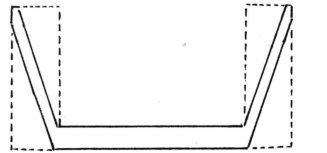

Fig. 13-7 Diagrams for hollowing ashtray blanks using core
drills. a) Top view showing
center cores of $\frac{1}{2}''$ (12.70mm)
and $\frac{3}{4}''$ (19.05mm), eight cores
of $\frac{1}{2}''$ (12.70mm) each, and
outer core of 2″ (50.80mm). b)
Side view profile. c) Side view
profile of finished ashtray.

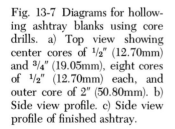

c

ting the aluminum. The disposable trays from TV dinners or supermarket pies furnish material of suitable thickness. The two foil pieces are then properly aligned and fastened to the gemstone blank with double stick tape. With this guidance, the placing of the drill hole locations, mostly done by feel, will not give too much trouble.

The drilling will take a while (maybe 15–20 minutes per hole), but since an automatic cam action drill is used, it need not impinge too much on the operator's time. The thing to do is to time the first hole (this timing is used as a gauge for timing the drilling of the other holes), and then check the drilling of each succeeding hole about a minute or so before this amount of time has elapsed. A kitchen timer will be quite helpful for this purpose. Thus, the operator can do other work around the shop while the drilling is going on. Each core should be broken out as it is drilled, inserting the wedge on the side on which the material is thicker than the plug to be removed. Reinsert each core in the hole from which it came. If the $1/2''$ (12.70mm) holes have been spaced very closely, there will be a fairly thick section of material left standing between the last and the first hole. In this case, the last and first holes can be filled with plaster of Paris and another hole drilled with this section as its center. This hole will go down very much faster since the drill will have only a very much smaller amount of gemstone to pierce. The new core, part plaster and part gemstone, is then broken out and the remaining plaster in holes one and seven chipped away, which is easy. The depth of all holes drilled up to now has been regulated with the homemade depth gauge.

6. Line up the work and deepen the $2''$ (25.80mm) ring which previously had been cut to only $1/8''$ (3.17mm) to its full depth of $1^1/4''$ (31.75mm).

7. Remove all core plugs one at a time. Measure them as they are taken out. If they are short of the desired depth, the hole has to be reamed out to the correct dimension using the nail, silicon carbide and water.

8. Undercut the ring between the $5/8''$ (15.87mm) and the $1''$ (25.40mm) groove.

9. Undercut the ring from which the $1/2''$ (12.70mm) holes were cut from its side toward the center of the preform until the cutting tool breaks into the holes. Then insert it in each hole and keep working until the pierced piece comes free. It is quite possible, and even likely that during the work, part of the structure to be undercut will break away, particularly if gemstone other than jade is used. This will call for some improvisation. It may, for example, be possible to remove some material by "knapping" with pliers and by chipping with the steel wedge. This may save some time.

There now remains a ring of gemstone $1/2''$ (12.70mm) wide around a cavity $1^1/4''$ (31.75mm) deep. The bottom of this will be somewhat lumpy unless a miracle has happened, and the next task is to get it perfectly even. This is a job to try a man's or woman's soul, and will teach anyone who undertakes it respect for the ancient cutters who had to do this sort of thing without electric motors and with sand as their abrasive. The best way I have been able to figure out to get this done is by use of the small homemade grinding wheels. Since these are laborious to manufacture and wear away fairly fast, I cast around for a second best way and came up with the alternate solution of employing the commercially-made $1^1/2''$ (38.10mm) grinders which are manufactured to be used in portable electric drills (see Fig. 13-8). The bond which holds the abrasive in these tools is too hard to work on gemstone, but they will serve very satisfactorily to carry loose silicon carbide grits mixed with water.

To obtain an even surface, the future ashtray is set loosely on the drilling platform, still wearing the collar which had been applied for the previous operations. A mixture of water and grit is put into the cavity. The drilling apparatus is then adjusted to work as a drill press, which means that the movable collar is moved up and fastened in place as high on the drill spindle as it will go. Then, the surface to be smoothed out is brought in con-

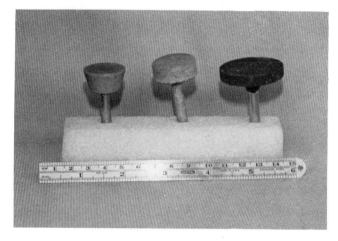

Fig. 13-8 Commercial silicon carbide tools used as grit carriers.

Fig. 13-9 Smoothing bottom of bowl.   Fig. 13-10 Shaping inside wall.

tact with the bottom of the milling tool by raising the drilling platform so that it touches firmly but does not "bind" (see Fig. 13-9). The blank is then rotated on the drill table, both in relation to the drill bit and around its own axis so that the tool can get in contact with every spot on the bottom of the small bowl. Very little pressure should have to be employed to keep the object moving, but it should not be possible to lift it. It is a good sign, if on being released momentarily, it starts to move ever so slightly. After a while, the effective contact will cease which means that a layer of material has been removed and the platform has to be raised a little. The work should be removed from the drill from time to time and cleaned enough to check its progress. The tool also should be inspected. It will be found that its working surface will be rounded somewhat. This should be corrected by grinding on one of the 8″ (203.20mm) wheels. The bottom of the bowl may be made either perfectly flat or slightly concave, at the discretion of the carver. (An alternative way of flattening the bottom of the ashtray or bowl is described in Chapter 14, when the treatment of the inset of the saucer is discussed.)

When the bottom is finished, the side walls which are now at right angles to the bottom are shaped (see Fig. 13-10). This, again, is best accomplished with the small homemade wheels. Before starting to work, the desired thickness of the sidewalls is marked on the rim with an indelible ink felt pen. The bowl is held by hand for this operation. The grinding is then started around the top of the inside border, keeping the stone moist by a little water in the bottom of the preform and a sponge applied whenever necessary. The piece is turned continuously to keep the cut even. As material is worn away at the top, the next lower level is worked, progressing gradually until the bottom of the ashtray is reached. This process is repeated until the inside wall slants evenly from the previously established bottom line to the felt pen mark. It will be found that bumps which may have been left in the side wall will be detected much more efficiently by feeling with the finger tips than by sight. The bottom of the preform is best protected during all this work by attaching a circle of aluminum to it with double stick tape.

We have now a bowl or ashtray with straight sides on the outside and a cavity slanting from 2″ (50.80mm) at the bottom to nearly 3″ (76.20mm) at the top. This is taken to the regular grindstones and the outside is shaped to conform to the inside contour. This does not mean that because the inside is round the outside also has to be a circle. Free rein is left to the imagination and skill of the carver. The illustration in the color section shows both a round bowl and one with an octagonal outline. This is accomplished by substituting octagonal outlines for both the top outside and the bottom circles in the original layout. It is not too hard to line up these shapes if it is done while the preform is still square.

Sanding is done first on the inside, beginning with Cratex wheels and proceeding to small wooden wheels with 600 grit. Wooden buttons (available in notion stores), epoxied to nails, are fine for this purpose. Polishing is done with muslin buffs or small felt wheels. On jade, a satisfactory polish is sometimes achieved by sanding. If much undercutting occurs, however, diamond compound on wood or hard felt may be needed. The outside may be sanded and polished on standard cabochon machinery.

Should a foot be desired on the bowl, it will be necessary to dop the bowl upside down, and center it again under the drill (see Fig. 13-11). Two core drills about ¼″ (6.35mm) apart in size are employed to demarcate the outside and inside of it to a depth of just less than ⅛″ (3.17mm). Then, the unwanted material of the inside of the smaller

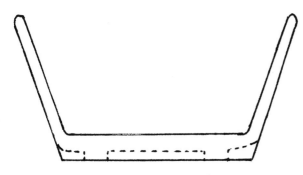

Fig. 13-11 Carving a foot for ashtray.

circle is ground away in an operation similar to the smoothing of the bottom on the inside of the ashtray. After this, the outside contours are established using the edge of a large grinding wheel. Sanding will have to be done for both surfaces, and the outside contour must be polished to harmonize with the texture of the rest of the exterior. The inside depression may also be polished to gild the lily.

After all this has been successfully accomplished, the carver will have to learn to suppress the impulse to commit mayhem on anyone rash enough to put ashes into his masterwork.

14
Making a Jade Cup and Saucer

For the cup and saucer two pieces of material are needed: one, 2″ (50.80mm) by 2″ (50.80mm) by 2³/4″ (69.85mm), and another one, ³/4″ (19.05mm) by 4″ (101.60mm) by 4″ (101.60mm). The former piece is for the cup, the latter for the saucer. These measurements are, of course, approximate and may be modified at will.

The first task after acquiring the gemstone is the making of exact layouts on paper showing a top view and a side view of each piece (see Fig. 14-1). A bottom projection is desirable, but not absolutely necessary. These drawings should show the dimensions and alignments which are required including the position of drill holes. The designs are then transferred to the gemstone blocks which, if very dark in color, may be first given a coat of white waterproof paint or layout ink (see Fig. 14-2). Then, a number of saw cuts are made which appear as dotted lines on the accompanying drawings (see Fig. 14-1a).

Making the Cup

In making the cup, first the two front corners are cut away (see Fig. 14-1b). Then, two ³/4″ (19.05mm) square pieces are sawn off; one on each side of where the handle is going to be. All the cuts made are at right angles to the top and bottom surfaces. The corners are sawed while holding the blank in a vise. To remove the two square pieces next to the handle, the block will have to be held by hand. These last two operations or, in fact, all the sawing may be postponed until all the drilling has been done, because the application of a collar to hold the drilling lubricant will then be easier. I prefer to do all possible sawing before starting to drill because the saw cuts might disclose some faults or weaknesses which would necessitate modifications of the project. After these six cuts, a seventh may be made establishing the underside of the handle (see dotted line in Fig. 14-1a).

Next, a collar made from decorator's or adhesive tape is applied to the blank, preliminary to hollowing out the cup. The drilling may be done with diamond core drills or regular metal drills in combination with silicon carbide. If both are to be used alternatingly, it is advisable to do all diamond drilling first. If this cannot be done, the silicon carbide mud must be carefully washed from the drilling area before diamond tools are resorted to, to avoid unnecessary wear on them. Diamond tools are a great boon in this and similar work since they do not require adjustment for shortening of the drill tube, which has to be figured for each hole bored with metal drills.

The interior of the cup is drilled in two stages. First come four $1/2''$ (12.70mm) holes, $1''$ (25.40mm) deep, arranged in the very center of the cup-to-be within a circle $1^{1}/_{4}''$ (31.75mm) in diameter (see Fig. 14-1b). These are broken out with a metal wedge. Then

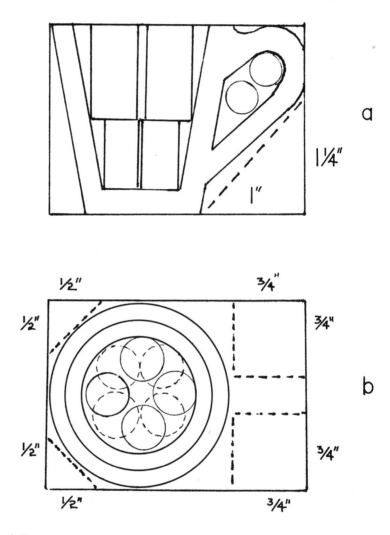

Fig. 14-1 Diagrams for drilling of cup: a) Profile sideview of cup showing arrangement for drilling, sawing, and shaping. b) Topview; secondary drilling holes, after first holes have been filled with plaster, are indicated by dotted circles. c) Layout of core holes for lower part of cup.

Fig. 14-2 Saucer and cup laid out with design transferred to the blanks.

a circular hole is drilled with a 1¼″ (31.75mm) core drill around the previous cuts, also 1″ (25.40mm) deep (see Fig. 14-1c). There will then be left a four-cornered wedge and four triangular ones around the periphery of the 1¼″ (31.75mm) circle. They can be removed by undercutting at their very bottom.

An alternate way would be to fill all the holes with plaster of Paris, and drill four additional holes mid-way between the plaster-filled cavities (shown in Fig. 14-1b by dotted circles) and, thereafter, remove the new cores by inserting the wedge between the outside walls and their gem portions. The plaster of Paris is used for filling holes previously cut because drills which are not supported all along their cutting surfaces, while in action, may "chatter." If the center has not been undercut, it may be broken out by covering it with a metal core drill just large enough to fit over it, which is then given a blow with a wooden or rubber mallet. This, with any luck, will snap it off cleanly. The bottom of the cavity, which is now 1″ (25.40mm) deep, is then flattened out and a new series of holes is started. The flattening before drilling does not have to be done too meticulously.

The new series of holes will have to fit into a circle ¼″ (6.35mm) smaller than the previous one. This means that only two holes will be drilled into solid gemstone, assuming that ½″ (12.70mm) core drills are employed. Before sinking the next two cuts, plaster of Paris will again have to be used. The new holes will have to be ¾″ (19.05mm) deep. A circle 1″ (25.40mm) in diameter will then be ground around them. All the sections of stone remaining in this hole will be so thin that they can be wedged out easily.

After this, the onerous task of reaming out the interior of the cup begins. The cup is held by hand throughout this operation. The procedure is much the same as the one described for hollowing out the small bowls. The best tools are, again, the small, homemade grinding wheels. The cutting should be done evenly, gradually going around the cavity numerous times to assure a uniform surface from top to bottom. Water is supplied by filling it into the cup which is moved up and down to keep the drill moist. Some splashing is unavoidable. A sponge may also be used to supply additional coolant.

As in the grinding of the bowl, a line drawn in indelible ink will help in establishing the thickness of the sidewalls. At first the work seems to get nowhere, but the fact that it will be necessary to wash the blank frequently to get rid of drilling mud will be an encouragement. After a while, it will be evident that progress is being made. It may be necessary to change the grinding bits from time to time as the largest possible tool is, of course, the best for speedy progress. If grinders in different grit sizes are available, the rougher abrasives should be used as long as possible, with the finest reserved for the final phase of shaping.

After the inside is finished, the exterior of the cup is formed. A piece of adhesive or decorator's tape, cut into a circle of the desired dimension, is placed to cover the bottom of the cup. The outside walls are then ground to the desired shape on the largest grinding wheels available. The sidewalls of the cup should be ⅛" (3.17mm) thick, or even less if the carver is courageous and jade is the material being used. Other materials will call for somewhat more solid walls to avoid complications.

After the cup proper has been brought to its final form, the handle is roughly shaped by sawing first (if this has not been done already), and then by grinding on the 8" (203.20mm) wheels. The thickness of the handle should be ⅜" (9.52mm) during the next operation which is drilling out its interior. Two holes are needed, one, ½" (12.70mm), and the other one, ¼" (6.35mm) in diameter. A piece of wood is fastened with dopping wax to the under side of the handle to minimize or, if possible, prevent splintering where the core breaks through the gem material. Then, a collar is put around the place to be drilled to retain the water if diamond cores are used, or the drilling mud if silicon carbide and metal core drills are employed. After the drilling, the inside of the handle is reamed out with Mizzy wheels. When this has been accomplished satisfactorily, it is shaped to the desired thickness of 3/16" (4.76mm) or a little less, and contoured on a well dressed grinding wheel. After this, all that is needed to finish the cup is a good sanding and polishing job. The inside of the handle may offer some little difficulties in sanding and polishing. Here, the techniques mentioned in Chapter 1 on "Sanding" procedure will come in handy. The wider part of the inside of the handle may be hand sanded with a piece of sanding cloth rolled on a short piece of doweling (see Fig. 14-3). The narrow end can be smoothed with a piece of picture wire charged with silicon carbide (see Fig. 14-4).

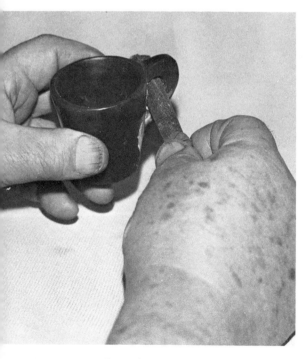

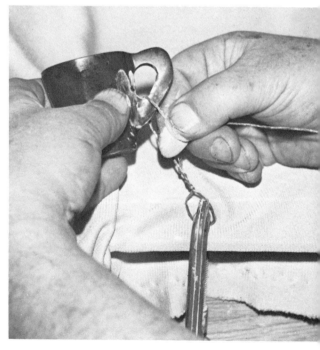

Fig. 14-3 Hand sanding of inside of cup handle.

Fig. 14-4 Picture wire charged with abrasive is used for sanding inside of cup handle.

Making the Saucer

The saucer is next. The slab from which it is to be made is painted on both sides with white paint or layout ink. An exact square with 4″ (101.60mm) sides is then outlined on one side, and the piece sawed or ground to these dimensions. Then, by drawing diagonals, the exact centers of both sides are established. After this, one of the surfaces is marked with a 4″ (101.60mm) circle and another concentric circle of the same diameter as the bottom of the cup (approximately 1½″—38.10mm). On the reverse side, another 4″ (101.60mm) circle is drawn in addition to a concentric one of the size desired for the bottom of the saucer (about 1¾″—44.45mm). All these lines are then redrawn for better visibility with an indelible ink felt tip pen.

The blank is next sawn to an octagon and thereafter ground to a circle (see Fig. 14-5). Then a circular incision is drilled into what will be the top of the saucer. If the slab is ³/₄″ (19.05mm) thick, this hole should be ½″ (12.70mm) deep. If a core drill of the correct size required to accommodate the bottom of the cup is available, all is well. Otherwise, a drill just a bit smaller will have to do. To contain the lubricant for this drilling, it is best to cut a collar (from an aluminum can or the waterproof cardboard from a juice can), only a little larger than the required hole. This is fastened to the slab with steel sash putty which, in turn, is affixed to the drill table with C-clamps. Following the drilling of the first larger circle, the interior of it is removed by sinking within it a series of closely spaced ½″ (12.70mm) holes to the same depth as the first one (Fig. 14-5). It is best to remove the small cores as drilled. The collar is then taken off, and the remnants of material within the small circular area are wedged out, leaving the bottom of the hole in a rather jagged condition.

Next, the blank is taken to a large, well-dressed wheel to grind out the inside contour. This may be a single concave line or a concave curve shallowing and leveling off toward the edges. The preform has to be turned continuously during this process to keep its shape even all around. (An aluminum template may be made to check accuracy.) Some of the protuberances of the rough spot in the center may be worn away during this operation. This is all to the good as long as the desired level of the center spot is maintained (see Fig. 14-5).

When all this has been satisfactorily accomplished, the bottom of the saucer is shaped to conform to the topside. It will save some time if some of the surplus gemstone is removed by sawing (see Figs. 14-6 and 14-7). For this purpose, the blank is held at a slant

Fig. 14-5 Top of saucer roughly shaped.

Fig. 14-6 The bottom of saucer presawed.

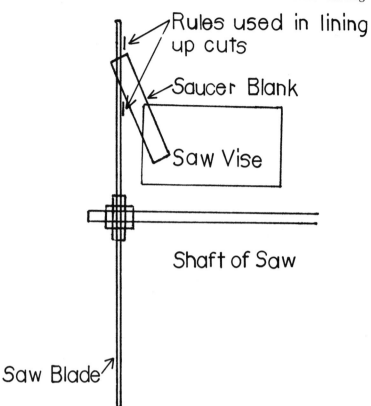

Rules used in lining up cuts

Saucer Blank

Saw Vise

Shaft of Saw

Saw Blade

Fig. 14-7 Diagram for sawing bottom of saucer.

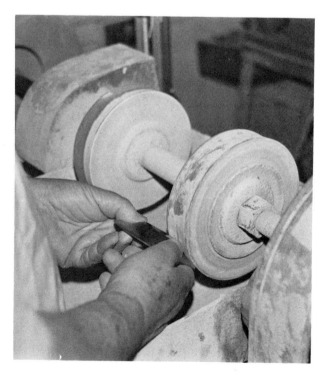

Fig. 14-8 A way for shaping bottom of saucer at right angle to the grinding wheel.

Fig. 14-9 A second method for shaping bottom of the saucer parallel to the grinding stone.

Fig. 14-10 Shaping cup inset.

in the saw vise. In order not to remove too much of the material, both top and bottom of each cut are carefully checked with a thin steel ruler held along the saw blade, as has been previously mentioned. The rest of the shaping is done by grinding.

Some of the curve on the underside of the saucer may be formed by holding the blank at right angles to the grinding wheel (see Fig. 14-8). It may even be possible to finish the operation in this manner if a well dressed wheel, worn down to a small enough diameter, is available. If a deeper curve than can be obtained in this way is needed, it will have to be ground on the edge of the wheel, holding the blank more or less parallel to the grinding stone (see Fig. 14-9).

After this, all that remains to be done now is to level off the center spot in the top of the saucer. For this purpose, a collar of tape is constructed around its rim, and it is set on the drill table without fastening or clamping it in any way. A homemade grinding stone is inserted in the chuck, and the drill adjusted so that it rests on the area to be flattened (see Fig. 14-10). The quill of the machine should be slightly elevated. A small amount of water is poured into the saucer and the machine started. The preform is rotated by hand so that the central indentation is evenly worn away. If a drill somewhat smaller than is needed to accommodate the bottom of the cup has been used to outline the center ring, a circle of the correct size should now be drawn on the blank using the bottom of the cup as a guide. Then, the indentation is enlarged to this line at the same time as it is evened out.

A good finish is a must on this piece, and the sanding and polishing will probably take nearly as long as the shaping of the set. A maple wood lap impregnated with 600 grit silicon carbide did most of the fine sanding on the cup and saucer pictured here. For the final polish, 14000 diamond grit compound on felt was used.

After finishing the cup and saucer, the carver will have only one problem: he will be expected to create five other identical ones to complete the set of demi-tasse cups.

15
Carving Jade Pendants

Making jade pendants is a very desirable exercise, preliminary to intaglio and relief cutting, in the use of small carving points as well as sanding and polishing tools with which to get into hard-to-reach recesses. Since one can never acquire enough of this skill, I recommend making more than one of these ornaments before going on to the next undertaking.

The examples shown here are an attempt to keep things as simple as possible, and are based mainly on drilling holes of various sizes and connecting them with saw cuts, followed by grinding with small carving points (preferably diamond charged) to shape the resulting pattern into pleasing contours. Since very little material is involved, only the best should be used. It may occasionally be feasible to arrange the work so as to cut away some undesirable flaws and inclusions by adjusting the design with this purpose in mind. It is a fascinating game to play around with a ruler, compass, and a template of circular patterns in various sizes to come up with a pleasing layout (see Fig. 15-1). The drill holes may vary from very tiny to $1/2''$ (12.70mm) and larger, and may constitute the major part of the design or may serve just as accessories to other work.

In the two very simple examples shown here, pieces of jade $2''$ (50.80mm) in diameter, and $3/8''$ (9.52mm) thick, were used. They were made from the blank cut out of the jade bracelet (Chapter 8). The leftover blank was dopped to a piece of wood and then sawn down the middle.

The simpler of the two pendants is made by drilling seven holes of identical size ($3/8''$—9.52mm—each) in addition to a smaller one (2mm) for attaching a jewelry jump ring and chain. One of these is in the exact center of the blank; the other six are spaced evenly around it with midpoints on a circle $1^1/4''$ (31.75mm) in diameter (see Fig. 15.2). The design may be executed directly on the blank which should be covered for this purpose with white layout ink if its material is too dark to show black lines clearly. Layout ink is recommended for this rather than paint, not only becuse it dries faster, but also because it does not discolor when heated. A template is used to outline the holes which should be

135

Fig. 15-1 Two possible designs for pendant.

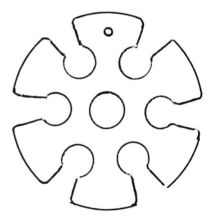

Fig. 15-2 Final design for pendant #1.

marked slightly larger than the outside circumference of the drill bits which are to do the work. This will help in lining things up later.

The preform is then dopped on a small piece of plywood. A collar of 1¹/₂″ (38.10mm) decorator's tape is constructed around it, which may be waterproofed further by a ring of putty around its base (see Fig. 15-3). The dopping wax should support the gemstone uniformly to minimize splintering where it is penetrated by the drill.

The holes can then be drilled one after another, cleaning up the work after each cut to facilitate the next one. Diamond core drills are very desirable for this work as the cleanup after each step is very easy since only water is needed as a lubricant. An improvised wooden gauge will help in determining the depth of each cut. When all holes

Fig. 15-3 Pendant blank dopped with collars of   Fig. 15-4 Jade blank with design dopped.
tape and putty.

including the 2mm one are drilled, the blank is released and two saw cuts made close to each other leading from the rim to each of the six holes. Then, the two surfaces of the medallion are modified so that the pendant can be worn with either side uppermost. The sharp edges are rounded off with Mizzy wheels or appropriate diamond tools, if such are available. A $1/2''$ (12.70mm) diamond-covered ball tool will be very helpful in the initial modification of the contours of each hole. The outer rim is shaped on a large grinding wheel. After sanding and polishing, a silver ring through the 2mm hole is all that is needed to make the pendant ready for wear.

The second pendant is a little more complicated. It is a simplified modification of an antique Chinese piece. It calls for a blank about $1^{1}/2''$ (38.10mm) by $2''$ (50.80mm), and $3/8''$ (9.52mm) thick. The other slice of the $2''$ (50.80mm) round from the inside of the bracelet may be used. Nine holes are required of three different diameters. The topmost is drilled with a $3/32''$ (2.38mm) core. All the others except the very center one which takes a $5/16''$ (7.93mm) core, are $3/16''$ (4.76mm) in diameter.

As with the previous pendant, the first step to take is the laying out of the design on the blank (see Fig. 15-4). Then the stone is dopped and equipped with a collar. A good way to do this is to fasten the preform to a thin piece of plywood (see Fig. 15-4) with dopping wax which should cushion the stone throughout. The preform is placed in a shallow dish slightly larger than the plywood backing. (The dish can be formed from an aluminum sheet, or a disposable pie dish, or similar material will do.) Then the dopped stone in the dish is clamped to the drill platform and water is added until its level is about $1/4''$ (6.35mm) above the object to be drilled (see Fig. 15-5). This arrangement permits easy adjustment from hole to hole. The various holes are drilled in any order the carver sees fit (see Fig. 5-6).

I found that on this project, cores on the inside of the drill often broke loose from the dopping wax and got stuck on the inside of the metal tubes. A long thin steel nail, or wire, or a knitting needle used with as little force as possible will usually nudge them loose without difficulty.

When all the perforating is done, the blank is released. All the necessary saw cuts are made and the shaping done, starting on the outside with the large grinding wheels

Fig. 15-5 Pendant to be drilled with aluminum   Fig. 15-6 All holes have been drilled.
reservoir.

and proceeding to the Mizzy and diamond points. This medallion, for variety's sake, is
shaped to be worn just one way.

Sanding on the pendants starts with Cratex points and wheels, progressing from
rougher to finer grits. For polishing, an assortment of small muslin buffs, felt wheels, and
leather disks of various sizes will be employed. Again, a ring of silver or gold wire,
depending on the chain on which it will be worn, will finish off the pendant.

16
Intaglio and Relief Carving in Hard Gem Material

There are two schools of thought on doing intaglio and relief carving. Beth Benton Sutherland, who was one of the few, and definitely the most erudite practitioner of the art in the United States, and who also wrote a book on it, is of the opinion that the work calls for years of apprenticeship and training. I have the good fortune of knowing one of her pupils who only partly shares her opinions. He insists that to do creditable work instruction is needed, and that in addition, one needs a special carving setup made just for this purpose and without any play in the bearings whatsoever. He did take some lessons confirming one part of Mrs. Sutherland's postulates; but refuting the "years and years" theory, he produced very fine work from the start of his involvement in the art and commenced to create excellent portraits in his first year of operations.

The other side of the question is represented by people like J. H. Howard in his *Revised Lapidary Handbook*, Gordon S. Kennedy in the *Fundamentals of Gem Stone Carving*, and Ed and Leola Wertz in their *Handbook of Gemstone Carving*, who, apparently, are of the opinion that we are dealing here with just another branch of gem carving which is accessible to, and possible for all and sundry, and may be undertaken with standard carving equipment.

The truth lies probably in the middle. Portrait and other highly refined work of this kind in hard gemstone does need specialization, both in the work itself and in the machinery used. Moderately skillful achievement is possible to anyone who is really interested. It is my personal opinion that superior performance in this branch of carving is reserved for a special few, endowed with more than usual talent, but that simple attempts, such as the ones described here, are possible and rewarding experiences for all who dare.

Before going into the matter any deeper, it is probably advisable to explain the terms used. *Intaglio carving* is the engraving of a picture in gemstone with the highest point of the subject being sunk deepest into the material. *Relief* is the opposite: a picture in three dimensions, sunk into gemstone, in which the highest point of the subject depicted is also most prominent. The dimensions of height or depth in both cases are greatly reduced in relation to the other two dimensions. The most suitable material to start with for intaglio and relief carving is plain transparent quartz (rock crystal), because it is abundant, relatively inexpensive, and works easily.

A third variant of this kind of carving should be mentioned here—*cameo carving*. This is a relief carving in gemstone with two or more straight parallel layers of contrasting color. One of these colors, usually the darker one, is used for background only, the other or others, for the image. Good material for this kind of work is hard to find, which is one of the reasons why most commercial cameos these days are cut from the multilayered King Helmet shell. It is also a good reason not to discuss cameo cutting here at all. Anyone who does have good material and is interested will have little difficulty entering the field if familiar with relief carving.

In this work it is of utmost importance, more so than in any other branch of gem carving discussed up to now, to have working conditions just right. The distance from the eye to the point of the carving tool is one important aspect in this picture. Good lighting is another; and a way to steady the hands so that they are both comfortable and still permit free movement of the object being carved in relation to the rotating tool point, is a third. Each carver will have to work out an optimum of these elements if he expects to be at all successful. An enlarging headpiece such as the Optivisor or clip-ons for eyeglasses, is very useful. Dependent on the height of the work table, it will probably be necessary to provide support for hands and forearms in the form of a small sturdy box, a chunk of planed lumber, or a stand made specifically for this purpose (see Fig. 16-1).

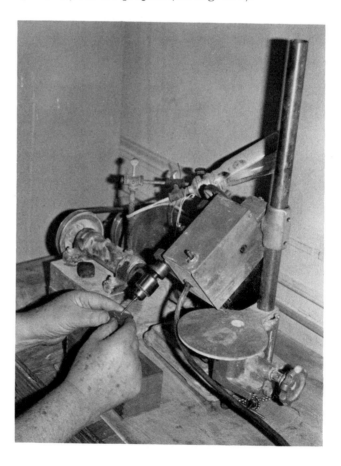

Fig. 16-1 The Pro-Carva drill set up for carving.

Also needed are suitable tools and designs. The professionals use steel points in dozens of shapes made on the same lathe which is doing the carving. When a situation calls for a specialized tool, it is made up on the spot. A mixture of viscous oil and diamond powders does the actual cutting. Amateurs are best served by diamond points made originally for various industrial uses, mostly for dental work. A well made diamond carving point is not cheap, but if treated right will last a long time; and for simple work, relatively few such tools are needed (see Fig. 16-2). Carving points are run either in a factory or homemade carving machine, or in a gem drill adapted for carving, or in a flexible shaft handpiece stabilized in a stand. The piece to be carved, if large enough, may be held by hand (see Fig. 16-1) or dopped to a block of wood about 2″ (50.80mm) by 2″ (50.80mm) by 2″ (50.80mm).

Few carvers will own the same set of tools and fewer still will agree on how exactly they will be utilized. I consider the following list of implements basic for small carving or engraving. The ones with an asterisk denote that they are useful but not absolutely needed. The whole set of eight would, at this time, cost about $75, the five essential ones costing about $30 to $35. This may seem like quite a lot of money, but they will last a long long time if properly cared for.

One lentil-shaped point, $1/8''$ (3.17mm) wide, $1/16''$ (1.58mm) thick.
One lentil-shaped point, $1/4''$ (6.35mm) wide, $3/32''$ (2.38mm) thick.*
One point, tapering from $1/32''$ (.79mm) at the top to $1/16''$ (1.58mm); length of taper, $5/32''$ (3.96mm).
One point, triangular in cross section; top $1/16''$ (1.58mm), decreasing toward shank to $1/32''$—.79mm—($1/16''$—1.58mm—high).
One point, triangular in cross section; top $1/8''$ (3.17mm), decreasing toward shank to $1/16''$—1.58mm—($3/32''$—2.38mm—high).*
One ball point, $1/16''$ (1.58mm) diameter.
One disk shape, $1/4''$ (6.35mm) diameter, $1/32''$ (.79mm) thick.
One small saw, $3/8''$ (9.52mm) diameter, $1/32''$ (.79mm) thick.*

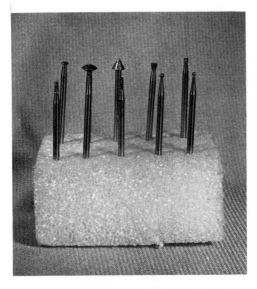

Fig. 16-2 Assortment of diamond carving points.

Fig. 16-3 A practice piece.

Before going to work in earnest, it is a good idea to practice (with whatever instruments are available) on scrap material or plain window glass, to get the hang of basic operations such as drawing straight lines or curves (see Fig. 16-3). One has to get accustomed to achieving these effects by moving the work instead of the scribing point. It will be found that it is best to barely touch the carving to the rotating point, carrying it back and forth along the lines intended in a very gentle and slow manner. Thus, if a mistake is made, it will be a shallow incision which is fairly easy to correct. Once a pleasing line is established, it is easy to achieve depth by going over it as often as needed. A foot-operated speed control, such as the ones which are practically standard equipment with flexible shaft tools, can be used on the carving head. This will also have the added advantage of enabling the carver to switch-start the machine and control the speed while supporting the work in both hands. The possibility of regulating speeds will also be helpful when sanding and polishing.

The best way to bring a water supply to the carving point is with a transfusion bottle (see Fig. 16-4). The outlet may either be attached to a stationary point of the drill (see Fig. 16-5), or to a finger of the carver by a contrivance made of wire (see Fig. 16-6)—copper being best as it is easily bent—to bring the drip exactly to the point where it is wanted.

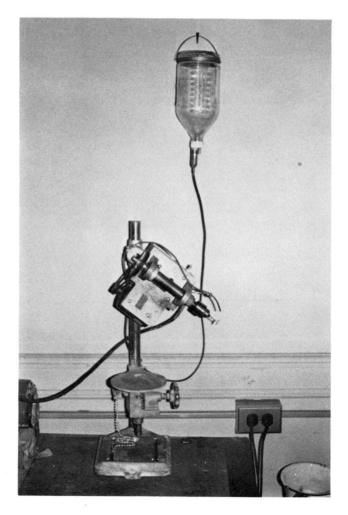

Fig. 16-4 Transfusion bottle used as water supply.

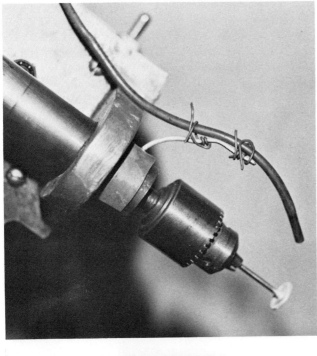

Fig. 16-5 Close-up of water supply arrangements.

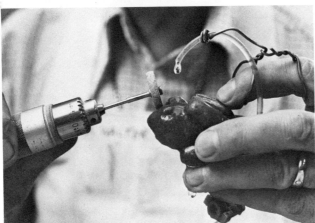

Fig. 16-6 Water supply attached to carver's finger.

All the arrangements having been made, we can now proceed to work. It is probably easiest to start off with an intaglio project. For this, a simple, yet attractive design is needed. For the first subject, a picture of a spray of tiger lilies was chosen. A slice of rock crystal about 3/8" (9.52mm) thick, 1½" (38.10mm) wide and 2" (50.80mm) high is the required material. The top and bottom of this slice should be parallel and without saw marks. If any are present, they should be ground away before any other work is started. This may either be done on the side of a grinding wheel, or on a piece of plateglass, but the surfaces should be neither sanded nor polished at this stage.

The design is then transferred to one plane thus prepared which should have the appearance of ground glass. Plain pencil is a good medium for the preliminary design until everything is just right. The final version is then traced with an aluminum point and retraced with a diamond stylus. The best tool I have found to do this is called "Lunzer's

Lancer." It is an implement looking like an automatic pencil, but it has a small pointed diamond where the graphite would ordinarily appear. The tracing should be repeated several times to establish a definite line which later can be followed by the rotary diamond tools. In using the diamond stylus, it is important to realize that hard pressure should not be used. Material is worn away by tracings repeated many times with very moderate force. Hard pressure may chip or even break the fine diamond point.

The first diamond point used is one with a very small lentil-shaped head with a sharp edge with which the previous diamond tracings are deepened. Then, the main stem of the flower is incised with a small ball-shaped tool which may also be used to do the deeper part of some of the flower petals. As has been stated already, it is impossible to give definite, clear instructions for the use of each point. If there are any doubts, the carver should experiment on a piece of scrap, and then transfer the acquired motion to the work in hand.

When the design seems complete, the quartz blank is ground to its final shape and all surfaces are sanded and polished. This treatment is not extended to the design itself which should have a neat and uniform finish imparted by the grinding points. It is best viewed through the uncut side of the quartz. If there are small corrections needed, they may be accomplished with the diamond scriber. Large flaws which become visible through the polishing of the surrounding areas may force a return to the rotary diamond points.

For someone who is new to this work, and sometimes even for someone who is not so new, it is practically impossible to cut clean lines all the time, and little nicks and places where the tool touched unintentionally are unavoidable. Many of these aberrations can be cleaned up by grinding away a thin top layer of the work surface after the image is well established (see Fig. 16-7).

The next project, a low relief or bas relief carving, should be preceded by extensive modeling in clay. Coins are good models for this work, with the English ones supplying fine examples of female heads and the American coins offering male portraits. It should be pointed out, however, that objects other than heads are perfectly legitimate subjects to be carved in low relief. A few flat slabs of Plasticine or similar materials are cut to practice on (see Fig. 16-8). The first few attempts should be considerably larger than the object

Fig. 16-7 Intaglio (tiger lily spray).

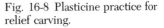
Fig. 16-8 Plasticine practice for relief carving.

which we are going to create—a man's head in profile. Small wooden modeling tools and smooth nail heads and needles pushed into pieces of soft wood as handles, are the instruments to work with.

As the carver is gaining experience, the image created can become smaller and smaller until a suitable one for the project is finally achieved. It might be a good idea to create a few tools from small nails similar to the diamond points available, and use these to make the final clay model.

When ready, a blank is chosen and prepared as in the intaglio project. Measurements can also be the same as there. Again, the image is outlined in a succession of pencil, aluminum, and finally, diamond stylus lines. Then, an oval line is drawn around the project, and stone is cut away between the outline of the image and the oval line in such a manner that the cuts are deepest next to the image and tapering off in depth as they reach the surrounding oval frame. For this work, a diamond tool, widest at the head and of a triangular profile, is very suitable.

Now the really difficult part of the work begins. The lines within the head proper are drawn as before and cut into the material very shallowly with a fine tapering diamond point. Here are some things to remember in the carving of a head in profile: The bridge of the nose is the lowest point of the image. The hair will have to be a little higher than the face. The eye should be a bit higher than the area immediately surrounding it. The ear is the highest point of all. Frequent use of two mirrors and use of the fingers on one's own head will be a good guide.

If at any stage the carver should be at a loss on how to proceed, a casting may be made of the present status of the work. A negative is produced first by pressing the carving into wet plaster of Paris. To keep it from sticking, the disk should be moistened with soap solution. When the plaster has set well, it is washed with the same soap solution and more wet plaster poured into the negative, thus creating a duplicate of the image so far created. This is removed from the mold and permitted to dry out well. More than one positive casting may be made if necessary. Then, corrections may be made on the cast by shaving it with a sharp tool. If they produce the desired effect, the corrections may be repeated on the quartz using the diamond tools.

When a satisfactory image is achieved, the whole design is gone over with Cratex

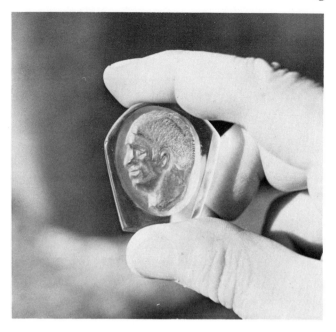

Fig. 16-9 Low relief carving of
man's head.

wheels and points to achieve a smooth surface (see Fig. 16-9). Some characteristic lines
may get lost in this operation and must be renewed. The frame of quartz is then sanded
and polished by conventional methods, being careful to stay away from the image proper.

A relatively small number of carvers will choose this branch of gem engraving as their
specialty, but everyone, in my opinion, should at least attempt it once or twice. It is not
as difficult as it seems.

Glossary

Abrasive Grits (powder): Small particles of hard substances used to shape metals, gemstones, or other hard materials by abrading.

Bead Gripper: A device making it possible to drill a bead from two opposite sides so that the holes will meet in a straight line.

Bead Mill: A device to grind and polish preformed pieces of gemstone into round beads.

Blank: A piece of gemstone sawn or ground to the approximate dimensions of the object to be carved from it.

Bow-drill: A drill which is activated by a string attached to bent pieces of wood.

Buff: Short for buffing wheel—a flat wheel pierced for running on shaft or spindle. It is commonly made of felt, layers of leather, or muslin, and is used to carry powders or mixtures for polishing.

Cabochon: A gemstone cut with one or more smoothly rounded surfaces.

Cam: An attachment which will lift and lower a drill spindle at regular intervals.

Cameo: A relief carving of a picture or design on gemstone which has differently colored layers. The contrasting colors are used to enhance the design.

Carbopol: A white powder manufactured by B. F. Goodrich Chemical Co. It is made into a jelly-like substance, useful in suspending, polishing, and grinding compounds.

Carver: 1) A person doing gem carving. 2) A machine used in gem carving.

Carving Shaft: The shaft of a rotary tool used for carving gemstone.

C-clamp: A device consisting of a C-shaped cast iron part and a screw, used to fasten two objects together.

Cerium Oxide: An oxide powder of the metal cerium, used for polishing gemstones.

Chrome Oxide: An oxide powder of the metal chrome, used in polishing gemstones.

Chuck: A device with adjustable jaws to hold a tool on a shaft or spindle.

Clip-on: An instrument fastened to another by metal clips.

Core Drill: A hollow metal tube used as a drill.

Cratex Wheels: Brand name of small (2″—50.70mm—or less) abrasive wheels.

Cutoff Disk: A small, round, thin disk made of abrasive grit, embedded in plastic, and pierced in the center.

Cylinder Seal: A design engraved on a small roller of gemstone, made to be impressed in wax or clay.

Diamond: A very hard crystal or carbon used for lapidary purposes in the form of fine powder which comes in many grades or particle sizes. It is used 1) in the form of a waxy and oily compound; or 2) bound to metal by plating, sintering, or imbedding (rotary saws, drill bits, drill cores, and cutting laps).

Dopping Wax: A compound similar to sealing wax, consisting mostly of shellac, used in fastening gemstones to wood or metal.

Dress: (A grinding wheel) Trimming a deformed grinding wheel to its correct shape.

Drill: An instrument for boring holes into hard substances. The drills used for gem drilling are usually electrically-driven, rotary drills, or drill presses.

Drill Chuck: See "chuck."

Drill Platform: The table on which rests the object to be drilled.

Drill Press: Drilling machine with a single vertical spindle.

Drill Quill: The tube-like bearing in which the drill revolves.

Drill Spindle: The revolving part of a rotary drill which holds the tool on one end in a chuck and a pulley on the other.

Faceting: Cutting a transparent gem with many flat surfaces.

Flange: A metal disk used in conjunction with a nut for clamping saws or grinding stones on a revolving shaft.

Flexible Shaft Tool: A device on which an electric motor and a grinding or polishing bit are connected by a flexible arm.

Gem Carving: The fashioning of gemstone by various abrasive and polishing tools into objects of art.

Gem Drill: A drilling device made especially for drilling gemstone, often equipped with a cam.

Gem Intarsia: A technique to create a picture or design from suitably shaped and finished pieces of gemstone.

Grindstone: A pierced, round disk of abrasive bonded in friable ceramic (in lapidary usage).

Grits: See "abrasive grits."

Grommet: An eyelet of metal or plastic used to reinforce a hole in fabric, leather, or similar material to prevent it from tearing.

Handpiece: In this book, usually refers to the grip by which a revolving tool is held.

Intaglio: A picture or design cut into gemstone in which the highest point of the depicted object is sunk deepest into the material.

Intarsia: See "Gem Intarsia."

Jacob's Chuck: Brand name of a special kind of chuck activated by a key.

Jig: A contrivance to hold pieces of material while being worked on in a machine.

Kerf: The slit or notch made by cutting instruments such as a saw.

Lap: A flat disk revolving horizontally to carry abrasive or polishing compounds; to cut with a lap.

Linde A: A finely graded corundum powder used for polishing gemstones.

Mandrel: A spindle: a working tool may be attached to its top by a setscrew.

Micrometer: A gauge permitting exact measurements to small fractions of a millimeter.

Mizzy Wheel: Brand name of very useful small (1"—25.40mm—or less) grinding wheels.

Optivisor: Brand name of a headband which holds magnifiying lenses in position in front of a worker's eyes.

Overhead Saw: A rotary gem saw on which the material to be sectioned is fed to the cutting blade below the axis on which it revolves.

Pellon: Brand name of a cardboard-like compression of plastic fibers used for polishing gemstone, especially flat surfaces.

Pillow Block: A cast iron or steel block with a hole in it to support a shaft.

Pipe Clamp: An attachment to a bench vise to hold a piece of pipe without deforming it.

Pipe Nipple: A short piece of plumbing pipe threaded on both ends.

Plastelena: Brand name of a non-hardening clay mixture.

Plasticine: Brand name of a non-hardening clay mixture.

Point Carving Tool: A device in which a carving or polishing tool is revolved by a small motor in the handpiece.

Polishing Mixture: A mixture of polishing powders and liquid.

Polishing Powder: A fine powder, usually a metal oxide, used for final smoothing of gemstones.

Polyhedron: A solid figure having many faces.

Preform: A piece of gemstone roughly shaped by sawing, grinding, or chipping.

Pulley: A wheel attached to a shaft over which a belt runs to connect two pieces of machinery.

Relief Carving: A picture or design carved into gemstone in which the dimension of depth is greatly reduced in relation to the other two. In this kind of carving the highest point of the object depicted is also the highest point in the carving.

Rip Fence: A device of wood or metal rigged exactly parallel to a saw blade to guide the material being cut.

Safety Goggles: A device to protect the eyes from flying debris.

Sanding Drum: A revolving wheel which holds belts of sanding paper or sanding cloth on its periphery.

Serpentine: A mineral (hydrous magnesium silicate).

Silicon Carbide: A synthetic made from silicon and carbon, used in loose powder form, or made up into grinding wheels, sanding cloth, or paper to work gemstones.

Slabbing Saw: A rotary saw with a diamond charged cutting blade, made to cut gem materials into sections.

Template: A flat shape of paper, plastic, wood, or metal, made to help shaping pieces of gemstone.

Tool Rest: An attachment to grinding machinery to hold steady a tool or piece of material while it is being applied to the cutting wheel.

Trimsaw: A rotary saw with a diamond-charged cutting blade made to cut small pieces or slabs of material into preforms.

Trysquare: A device made for testing right angles.

Tub Machine: A lapidary machine, the body of which is a flat tub in which a vertical spindle operates horizontal cutting or polishing laps.

Undercut: Irregular wearing away of material during the finishing process.

List of Suppliers

Materials and machine supplies for carving are getting easier to buy from day to day. As more people take up the work their needs are more widely catered to. If there is a local rockstore, it will be best to shop there first. Annually, the April issue of the *Lapidary Journal* (*The Rockhound Buyers Guide*) is the next best source for finding what one needs. It lists in alphabetical order as well as by state location, the names of most dealers in the United States. There is also an alphabetical index of products which gives the names of the dealers who carry them. I shall, therefore, enumerate here only the names of dealers and manufacturers who specialize in carving and drilling equipment, and who sold the material and supplies used in this book.

Baskin and Sons
732 Union Avenue
Middlesex, NJ 08846
   One of the few dealers carrying good jade in the East.

Aubrey E. Cole
330 Sherwood Drive N.E.
Vienna, VA 22180
   A carver of distinction himself, Mr. Cole specializes in carving tools.

Covington Engineering
112 First Street
Redlands, CA 92373
   Manufacturer of an automatic gem drill and a drill carver, and other gem cutting machinery.

Crown Manufacturing Co.
575 "F" N. Twin Oaks Valley Rd.
San Marcos, CA 92069
   Producers of the Pro-Carva Drill, Bead Gripper, Rohlane Carver, and many other drilling and carving tools.

Dremel Mfg. Division
Emerson Electric Co.
4915-21st Street
Racine, WI 53406
   Manufactures a line of hand-held carving tools, a flexible shaft tool, and some stands to convert these into small drill presses.

Foredom Electric Co., Inc.
Bethel, CT 06801

Manufactures the most widely used flexible shaft and accessories.

Frances Paul Enterprises
3033 La Madera Ave.
El Monte, CA 91732

Formerly a manufacturer, now only sells carving and drilling equipment and supplies.

Gemart by Charles (Chas. W. Perry)
3607 S. El Camino Real
San Clemente, CA 92672

Supplied the material for the spheres.

Geode Industries,
106–108 West Main, Highway 34
New London, IA 52645

Makers of the Viking Gem Drill.

Grieger's Inc.
900 So. Arroyo Parkway
Pasadena, CA 91109

Offers a wide selection of books, gem materials, and other supplies in its Pasadena store and by mail order through its excellent catalog.

Highland Park Manufacturing
12600 Chadron Ave.
Hawthorne, CA 90250

Manufactures a wide line of gem cutting equipment, particularly a good selection of saws. They have recently added a sturdy gem drill to their product line.

Lunzer Industrial Diamonds, Inc.
48 West 48th Street
New York NY 10020

Furnished all the diamond core drills and most of the carving points for the projects described.

P.D.Q. Lapidary Manufacturing Co.
P.O. Box 75411
Oklahoma City, OK 73107

Maker of the P.D.Q. Gem Drill.

Technicraft Lapidaries
2248 Broadway
New York NY 10024

The only place in New York City where a wide line of carving and other lapidary equipment is on display. Seller of the jade used for the necklace.

Bibliography

Ball, Sidney H. *Roman Book of Precious Stones.* Los Angeles: Gemological Institute of America.

Cellini, Benvenuto. *Autobiography.* Translated by J. Addington Symonds. New York: Walter J. Black, Inc.

Cottrell, Leonard, and Davidson, Marshall. *Lost Worlds.* New York: American Heritage Publishing Co.

Desautels, Paul. *The Gem Kingdom.* New York: Random House.

Gump, Richard. *Jade: Stone of Heaven.* New York: Doubleday & Co., Inc.

Hahn, Emily. *The Diamond.* New York: Doubleday & Co., Inc.

Hansford, S. Howard. *Chinese Carved Jades.* Greenwich: New York Graphic Society Ltd.

Hansford, S. Howard. *Chinese Jade Carving.* Greenwich: New York Graphic Society Ltd.

Howard, J. Harry. *Revised Lapidary Handbook.* Greenville: Published by author.

Howell, F. Clark. *Early Man.* New York: Time-Life Books.

Kennedy, Gordon S., et al. *The Fundamentals of Gem Stone Carving.* San Diego: The Lapidary Journal.

von Koenigswald, C. H. R. *Meeting Prehistoric Man.* New York: Harper & Brothers.

Kunz, George Frederick. *Gems & Precious Stones of North America.* (reprint) New York: Dover Publications Inc.

Obermaier, Hugo. *Der Mensch Der Vorzeit.* Berlin: Allgemeine Verlags-Gesellschaft.

Palmer, J. P. *Jade.* London: Spring Books.

Piggott, Stuart. *The Dawn of Civilization.* New York: McGraw-Hill Book Co.

Polo, Marco. *The Travels of Marco Polo.* Translated by Wm. Marshden. New York: Dell Publishing Co.

Pond, Forrest W. *How to Make and Use Gem Carving Tools.* Santa Ana: Published by author.

Quick, Lelande, and Leiper, Hugh. *Gemcraft.* Radnor: Chilton Book Co.

Schubnel, Henry Jean. *Gems & Jewels.* New York: Golden Press.

Sinkankas, John. *Gem Cutting: A Lapidary's Manual.* Princeton: D. Van Nostrand Co., Inc.

Sperisen, Francis J., *The Art of the Lapidary.* Milwaukee: Bruce Publishing Co.

Sutherland, Beth Benton. *The Romance of Seals and Engraved Stones.* New York: Macmillan Co.

Tavernier, Jean Baptiste. *Travel in India.* Translated by V. Ball. London: Macmillan Co. (1889).

Wertz, Ed and Leola. *The Handbook of Gemstone Carving.* Mentone: Gembooks.

Whitlock, Herbert P. *The Story of Gems.* New York: Garden City Publishing Co.

Woolley, C. Leonard. *Digging up the Past.* New York: Chas. Scribners Sons.

MAGAZINE ARTICLES

The following list is as complete as I could make it. Many of the *Lapidary Journal* articles prior to February 1967 have been reprinted in the book *Fundamentals of Gem Stone Carving,* which was compiled and written by Gordon S. Kennedy, and which I cannot recommend highly enough. If the back numbers listed cannot be found in the reader's library or in that of their friends, some will be available through the respective magazines. Not all the pieces listed are "how to" instructions, but all contain valuable references and information.

Gems & Minerals, P.O. Box 687, Mentone, CA 92359.
Beck, Howard K. "Models of Stone": April 1973.
Bird, Milo A. "Cutting Unique Trays and Bowls": January 1967.
"Drilling Gemstones," from *Gem Cutters Handbook:* March 1965.
Lundall, Virgil V. "How to Turn Gem Stone Bowls": March 1970.

Lapidary Journal, P.O. Box 80937, San Diego, CA 92138.
Barnett, W. P. "Obsidian Carving": March 1967.
Cole, Aubrey E. "A Gemstone Carving Project for the Beginner": July 1970.
———. "To Carve a Cat": June 1968.
Colhour, Olive. "El Picaro, A Florentine Mosaic": April 1968.
———. "Red Huckleberries": April 1971.
———. "So This Is Obsidian": April 1967.
Dale, Neil. "The Process of a Gem Carving": June 1974.
Gibbs, Shirley. "How to Make a Sphere": April 1966.
Gross, W. G. "Carving a Jade Bowl": May 1966.
Harris, David S. "Ashtray Maker": August 1972.
Heinz, W. W. "Intarsia, That Strange Name": December 1971.
Hobby, A. Worth. "Creative Carving": September 1962.
———. "Figure Carving of Gem Plates": November 1965.
———. "The Use of Soft Steel Grinding Heads in Carving Jade Dinner Plates": April 1965.
Logan, Howard. "A Connecticut Yankee Revives an Ancient Art": November 1970.
Longnecker, Paul. "Searching for an Idea": May 1973.
———. "Small Carvings": October 1971.
Maline, Maurice. "New Carvings": September 1973.
Mazze, Beverly. "The Making of a Gem Engraver": June 1973.
McConnell, C. L. "A Procedure for Intarsia": July 1968.

Neavitt, Tom. "About Bead Making": July 1968.
———. "About Carving": August 1967.
———. "About Making Gem Beads": January 1968.
———. "Making a Jadeite Perfume Bottle": July 1969.
Parser, Donald. "How the Japanese Cut Gemstone": April 1962.
Peterson, Wilma J. "Mushrooms, Texas Style": September 1973.
Schutt, Aline. "Sculptured Obsidian Head": June 1972.
Seitz, Martin. "The Intaglios of Martin Seitz": May 1966.
Sims, Charles. "A Carving Machine": October 1972.
———. "Carving a Rose": December 1970.
Smith, John H. "Commercial Gem Carving in Japan": March 1965.
Zeitner, June Culp. "Quartz Intaglios Revisited": September 1971.
———. "Stones in Bloom": February 1972.

Rock and Gem, 16001 Ventura Blvd., Encino, CA 91316.
Cole, Aubrey E. "Why Not Try Carving": May 1972.
Hadley, Wayne D. "Goblets of Gemstones": October 1973.
Jones, Robert W. "Curious About Carving": July 1973.

Index

Photograph by Viola Finger

I was born in 1906, grew up and was educated in Munich, Germany. After graduation, I went into the hotel business. After stints of working in Italy, Switzerland, and Egypt, I came to the United States in 1928. Here, I had to work up the ladder once more from dishwasher, busboy and waiter, to managerial positions. In 1940 I married, being very very fortunate in the choice of a wife, and am the proud father of two sons. Stones interested me from an early age, but I didn't do anything about it until 1946 when I became a member of the New York Mineralogical Club. In 1950 my allegiance switched to the Lapidary and Gem Society of New York which was then a year old. I served this organization in all the offices including repeated terms as president. I learned cutting gemstones in courses given at New York University in the early fifties and have been at it ever since. In 1959, I became one of the lapidary instructors at the Craft Students League—a branch of the Y.W.C.A. In 1965, I was chairman of the Eastern Federation of Lapidary and Mineralogical Societies Show; the first such affair ever held in New York City. In 1971, I retired after twenty-five years as manager of a large hotel in New York. My first book, *Gem Cutting Is Easy*, came out in the spring of 1972. Articles of mine have appeared in several magazines, mostly in the *Lapidary Journal*.